SOUL BEGINNINGS

ILLUMINATING GENESIS 1-11

MARK FORREST

SOUL BEGINNINGS

ILLUMINATING GENESIS 1-11

Cotton Foster
940-682-5292

MARK FORREST

Partner with SycamoreTreePress.com

It's good to be Zacchaeus and have Jesus to your house for tea,
It's better to be the Sycamore tree and lift others up to see.

ENDORSEMENT

"Dr. Mark David Forrest has finally placed in written form one of the fantastic sermon series for which he is properly recognized as a premier contemporary expositor of Holy Scripture. In Soul Beginnings, Dr. Forrest returns the reader to the beginning of time. He draws back the curtain of history to show us not only that the biblical text is trustworthy, but that it holds important truth for you as a human being today.

These eleven sermons on Genesis 1-11 will enlighten your mind by surveying the grand vista of the cosmos, just as they will lift up your heart by offering the gospel hope of personal transformation."

~Malcolm B. Yarnell III, Author of God the Trinity and The Formation of Christian Doctrine, and Research Professor at Southwestern Seminary in Fort Worth, Texas

DEDICATION

To my faithful, loving wife of 30 years, Gina—my treasure and my rock.

To our children—Emily, Madison, Caroline, Seth, Luke, and Olivia—who have helped make life lessons possible.

I am deeply humbled and grateful for my family—my heroes.

Editor's Note:

Dr. Mark Forrest writes as he preaches—for everyday people—those of us who have questions, make mistakes, and long for God's grace. In Soul Beginnings, Mark gives biblical wisdom for living and introduces the very heart of God—showing how the Uncreated created. In the Introduction Mark shares his story with transparency. In small bites, you will find the first and second creation story, get a glimpse of the relationships God ordained and find the plan for a Savior in the Garden of Eden.

For those who are blessed each week by hearing Mark's teachings, this book can cement into your hearts God's word. For the rest of you, this book can usher you into the presence of God, through the Power of the Holy Spirit. It's my hope that you grow in your faith as my husband and I have while learning from Mark. May the Holy Spirit open your eyes, heart and mind.

Peggy Purser Freeman
Editor, freelance writer and author
www.PeggyPurserFreeman.com

CONTENTS

Acknowledgments   x

Introduction   xii

1   His Story is My Story   1

2   It is Good Not to Be Alone   15

3   Broken   27

4   East of Eden   43

5   A Radical God   59

6   God's Broken Heart   73

7   Creation 2.0   89

8   God Remembers   105

9   God's Covenant   117

10   More Begats   129

11   Tower of Power   141

About the Author   155

ACKNOWLEDGMENTS

Throughout the process of studying, writing, and preaching this story, I have been utterly impressed with the Father's graciousness for surrounding me with a "living hedge" of precious people. I feel so blessed.

To my loving and faithful wife, Gina, you are a product of God's grace who was influenced by godly parents, siblings, and friends. I believe we have accomplished more together, as a team, than we could ever do alone.

To our children, I am so proud of each of you: Emily and her husband Cameron, Madison, Caroline, Seth, Luke, and Olivia. Jesus has shined brightly through you. We have jokingly called you all, "Daddy's little sermon illustrations." But you each have really taught me what the important things in life are.

To our church families, I thank Liberty Baptist Church for giving me an opportunity to pastor when I didn't know if anyone else would. The challenges at this little church were great in a tough neighborhood, but I learned some real-life lessons. I thank Murphy Road Baptist Church for giving me a place to raise my children and learn how to really grow a church and grow with a church. When I wasn't sure if I could even be a pastor, you all let me thrive. I thank Lakeside Baptist Church for giving me a place not only to be a pastor but become a leader. In all of these places we've called home, they have taught me more than I taught them.

To my pastors and ministry assistants, thank you for supporting me in the good times and in the bad times. I go to work every day knowing that I am loved and appreciated. Your patience, time, love, and encouragement have helped make this humble offering more acceptable.

My words seem inadequate to express the deep gratitude I

feel for Peggy Freeman's help.   Your writing expertise, organization, and loving encouragement along the way have indebted me to you.

Thank you to Preston Cave and Lana Robinson for suggestions and prayers.

Cover Credit:
Brandon Cave
www.hellohealey.com

Healey
DESIGN & PHOTO

And lastly, I want to thank all of you who will dare to be readers and process the life lessons that came to my heart so powerfully. Please be quick to obey all that our Lord says to you. I love you and thank the Lord for you.

Introduction

In the Fall of 2016, my chest contracted in pain, I tried to relax, to breath, to ignore. The pains grew more intense, lasted longer, and when I thought I had overcome the pains, they happened, again and again, growing closer together. My fear made them worse. Doctor appointments were made, tests planned.

"My dad passed away with a heart attack when he was just fifty years old," I told our doctor. Even though my dad had other health issues, I worried that I would repeat the same fate at forty-nine.

My family doctor sent me to a cardiologist and the tests revealed some blockage. He scheduled an angiogram, and I anticipated needing a stint or two to clear up the issue. As I came out of my haze from the anesthesia, I heard, "Good news, there was no blockage." I cried tears of relief and knew the Lord had mercy on me.

Providentially, my church had given me a two-month sabbatical. With the unexpected time off and a clean bill of health, I knew I had to do something productive. Maybe I could write a book or preach at a small church in the country. I also had learned to better deal with stress to keep those chest pains from returning.

Change became mandatory. But how do I make change permanent? Engrafting is used in horticulture to place part of one plant on to the root or branch of another plant to incorporate in a firm or permanent way. This helps strengthen plants, create resistance to disease, to ensure pollination, and to adapt to environments. (2) If we were to take this principle and apply it to our spiritual walk, what would we want to incorporate into our lives in a permanent way to strengthen us?

Most of us would want to know how to apply the truths in the

Bible in a real way. How would your life be different if you knew how to make Scripture a permanent part of your journey? This became my focus.

The answer came out of necessity when I had a meltdown. I vocalized walking away from everything and doing something else with my life. I had always struggled with insecurity which led to passive-aggressive behaviors that I thought I could handle privately. This time it became a revelation that I needed help. I needed to incorporate some things in my life, and I started with counseling, Celebrate Recovery (1) and reading as many books as I could on anger, faith, love, family, and recovery. Having been in the ministry for over half my life, I felt like I needed to revisit every sermon I had ever preached. I needed to really learn how to apply what God had given me the privilege to study as a pastor for many years. Change was needed, but I wanted it to be permanent.

Both in counseling and working the steps in Celebrate Recovery, I had to go back to the beginning of my life and do an inventory. Step four in recovery is called taking a "fearless inventory." This led me to preach a series on the beginning in Scripture. Not only did I begin to sense a real healing in my soul, but I also sensed a new idea of my worth to God. Yet, there were some things I needed to re-apply to my life if I wanted it to stick. I sensed a desperation when it came to my recovery. This time would be different. This time I began a journey to see who God says I am.

CHAPTER 1
HIS STORY IS MY STORY

On Christmas day, 1968, the three astronauts aboard Apollo 8 rounded the dark side of the moon. Immersed in the darkness, as they turned to begin their trek home, that awe-inspiring sight appeared. The bright blue and white swirl of our earth rose above the moon's darkened horizon.

These men, trained in science and technology, didn't talk about Galileo, Hubble, or Einstein. Their first inclination wasn't singing a song, reciting a poem, or wishing everyone on earth a Merry Christmas. Only one thing could capture this awe-inspiring moment(3) of viewing earth from space—the first verse of the first chapter of Genesis.

"In the beginning God created the heavens and the earth." Genesis 1.1 (NKJV)

The book of Genesis is the first book in the Bible for a reason. It's a really, really important book. It tells us who we are, where we're going, and who we are meant to be.

The New Testament refers to the book of Genesis about 200 times, and half of those references are to the first eleven chapters of Genesis. Jesus Christ quoted or referred to each of the first seven chapters of Genesis. These opening chapters of the Bible show us God's intention for humanity.

You are Part of God's Story

"In the beginning God created the heavens and the earth." Genesis 1.1 (NIV)

These ten words are how it begins and they are the most quoted words in all of literature. If you believe this verse, you will have little trouble believing the rest of the Bible. God is the theme of Genesis 1. He is mentioned 35 times in 31 verses. All things exist by Him, for Him, and through Him. These ten words, translated from only seven Hebrew words, are filled with incredible meaning.

In the Beginning, the Uncreated God Created

God did not begin—He has always been. This is the ultimate explanation for the beginning of all things. Moses wrote this account just after the Exodus. Some believe it was borrowed. However, none of the neighbors of Israel held this same view of God. Their pagan gods had long family trees and their gods would steal the wives of other gods. Therefore, the idea that the Biblical creation story was borrowed from other cultures is completely unfounded.

God was Solely Responsible for Creating

In Scripture, the word "create" is only used to describe the actions of God and only used to describe the action of producing something new.
1. God Himself is the one creating.
2. The word "create" is never used with any reference to the materials used.
3. God only had to speak. The Latin term used is *ex nihilo*—meaning, "out of nothing."

Genesis paints a picture of this as the special focus of God's creation.

An accurate translation would be: "In the beginning God

created the heavens and **especially** the earth." This reminds us how extraordinary our earth is and therefore, how special we are to God.

God Changes Chaos into Cosmos

Some scholars struggle with interpreting Scripture with supernatural meaning. Yet, a Creator God can speak this universe into existence can do anything from changing hearts to healing hurts.

Take this example in the Gospel of Mark:
"Teacher, I brought you my son, who is possessed by a spirit that has robbed him of speech. Whenever it seizes him, it throws him to the ground. He foams at the mouth, gnashes his teeth and becomes rigid..." When the spirit saw Jesus, it immediately threw the boy into a convulsion. He fell to the ground and rolled around foaming, at the mouth." Mark 9:17-18, 20 (NIV)

What medical condition does that sound like? Epilepsy. People have said over the years that in Biblical times, there was no science and people needed religion to explain strange things, like saying it was a demon. I don't think that's what's going on at all in this passage. I think it was demonic, but that's what people say sometimes. Therefore, scientists reason that religion is an attempt to explain things for people who didn't know any better. They also reason that Genesis 1 is another example of that. Is it something we can no longer trust because science has taught us better? Often the conflict between science and faith comes from a misreading of the Bible.

Structure of Genesis Chapter One

Day 1 Day, Night

Day 2 Sky, Waters
Day 3 Land, Plants
Day 4 Sun, Moon, Stars
Day 5 Birds, Fish
Day 6 Animals, Humans
Day 7 Sabbath, Completed

The first three days involve days of forming, and the corresponding 4th, 5th, and 6th days are days of filling.

Moses gives us a poetic description of creation. Hebrew poetry is based on repetition rather than rhymes.

Repetition in Genesis Chapter One

"...and God said..." (vv. 3, 6, 9, 11, 14, 20, 24, 26, 28, 29)

"...let there be..." (or some form thereof; vv. 3, 6, 9, 11, 14, 20, 24, 26)

"...and it was so..." (vv. 3, 7, 9, 11, 15, 24, 30)

"...and God made..." (or similar action; vv. 4, 7, 12, 16, 21, 25, 27)

"...and God saw that 'x' was good..." (vv. 4, 10, 12, 18, 21, 25, 31)

Some form of naming or blessing (vv. 5, 8, 10, 22, 28)

"...there was evening and there was morning..." (vv. 5, 8, 13, 19, 23, 31)

A designation of the day as first, second, etc. (vv. 5, 8, 13, 19, 23, 31; 2.2)

No other chapter in Genesis is written in such a poetic way. Most of the prophets in the Old Testament preached and wrote in a poetic style. It doesn't mean it's not true; its true, but Genesis was written so that it would stay with us. It wasn't written as a science book, but as a love letter, or better yet, a song written for us and about us. You must be careful about dissecting these passages as if it were a textbook.

Ancient Near East Myths

Most cultures in Moses' day were polytheistic (belief in many gods). These gods were chaotic and impersonal. Therefore, life in these cultures was this constant exercise of trying to appease the gods. They had versions of a creation story. However, none of the other accounts of creation mention God's goodness and His promises. Genesis 1 subverts the lies of these other gods.

Examples of the contrasts:
- In the pagan accounts, the creatures in the sea are gods and they are chaotic. ↔ In the Genesis account, the creatures in the sea are just creatures.
- Pagan cultures worshiped the sun, the moon, and the stars, ↔ The Genesis account calls them lesser and greater lights.
- In the pagan accounts, humans are created as an afterthought to relieve the gods of work. ↔ Human beings are not created as an afterthought in Genesis. In Genesis, humanity is the very goal of creation. And God's first communication to them is a blessing that they are made in God's image.
- In the historical time this account was written, it addressed real issues, but the issues of the day weren't Darwinism or modern science. Genesis 1 and 2 are **not** primarily concerned with **how** God made the world, but **that** God made the world.

Controversy of Understanding Genesis One

"The question is—if it's poetic, then how are we to read it?"

"'Let there be light,' and there was light." Genesis 1:3 (NIV)

What light is this? Remember this was written in a time when people worshiped the sun, moon, and stars.

On the fourth day: "God made two great lights—the greater light to govern the day and the lesser light to govern the night. He also made the stars. God set them in the vault of the sky to give light over the earth... And God saw that it was good. And there was evening and there was morning—the fourth day." Genesis 1:16-19 (NIV)

How could there be light because the sun doesn't show up until the fourth day? Again, the point is more spiritual than scientific.

Question: *Who is the light of the world?*
Answer: *God. God is light.*

He can light the world with or without the sun. I heard a preacher once declare that the most important phrase in Scripture is "Let there be light." It specifically addresses the pagan belief of worshiping the sun. God is the source of all things, not the sun.

Is it Possible to Reconcile Genesis 1 with Modern Science?

George Henri Lemaitre was the first to propose that the universe was expanding (two years before Edwin Hubble). He was a world-class astronomer and physicist, but also a priest. He proposed what is known as the Big Bang Theory. Back then, most people rejected this theory because a Christian suggested it. Every scientist though, knew its implication: that everything had a definite beginning. They believed, as some do even now, that the universe was eternal.

Some of these scientists have moved me to greater faith because they have shown how science and faith don't necessarily have to be enemies. One example of this is from Dr. Fritz Schaefer:

> "The significance and joy in my science come in the occasional moments of discovering something new and saying to myself, 'So that's how God did it!' My goal is to understand a little corner of God's plan." - Dr. Fritz Schaefer, Graham Perdue Professor of Chemistry and Director of the Center for Computational Quantum Chemistry at the University of Georgia. (4)

No matter what you believe, the real question is whether it all began personally or impersonally. Either way you believe, you are exercising faith.

Was it all just from a speck? "In the beginning was a speck." Or was there a thoughtful plan? I don't have enough faith to believe in the speck. The believer in the speck has to reason from the lesser to the greater. I choose to reason from the greater to the lesser.

Another physicist, Dr. Patrick Glynn, abandoned atheism for Christianity because he understood the implications of the Big Bang.

Dr. Glynn, the Associate Director and Scholar-in-Residence at the George Washington University Institute for Communitarian Policy Studies said:

> "Ironically, the picture of the universe bequeathed to us by the most advanced twentieth-century science is closer in spirit to the vision presented in the book of Genesis than anything offered by science since Copernicus." - Dr. Patrick Glynn, (5)

Even renowned atheist, Dr. Stephen Hawking begrudgingly admits:

>"So long as the universe had a beginning, we could suppose it had a creator."- Dr. Stephen Hawking (6)

Once Einstein understood the universe is expanding, he moved from agnosticism to believing in God and said of his ultimate desire:

>"...to know how God created this world...I want to know his thought. The rest are details." Dr. Albert Einstein (7)

On April 24, 1992, scientists discovered the Big Bang ripples using NASA's COBE and many said it was like looking at the fingerprints of God.

>"These findings, now available, make the idea that God created the universe a more respectable hypothesis today than at any time in the last 100 years." - Frederick Burnham, Science-historian (8)

And finally, my favorite quote:

>"For the past three hundred years, scientists have been scaling the mountain of ignorance, and as they pull themselves over the final rock, they are greeted by a band of theologians who have been sitting there for centuries."- Dr. Robert Jastrow, an agnostic and founder and director of the Goddard Space Center. (9)

More scientists are converting from atheism than at any other time in history.

There Are No Such Thing as Mere Mortals

"Then God said, "Let us make mankind in our image, in our likeness, so that they may rule over the fish in the sea and the birds in the sky, over the livestock and all the wild animals,[a] and over all the creatures that move along the ground." Genesis 1:26 (NIV)

At the close of chapter one, notice the difference in the wording. Every other day there was a pattern: "God said... and it was good." But here He says, "Let us make man..." Because He's God, He knows everything—right? He knows this man and this woman will disobey; He knows that sin will be passed from generation to generation. He knows that to remedy this problem He will have to offer His own Son on a Roman cross. Yet, knowing all of that will happen, He creates them anyway.

This tells us we are worth it to Him.
> "There are no ordinary people. You have never talked to a mere mortal... Next to the Blessed Sacrament itself, your neighbor is the holiest object presented to your senses."- C. S. Lewis (10)

Everyone matters to God because we were all made in His image. James 3:9 warns us not to curse people because they are made in His image. This is why Christians have always valued life.

We sent the Mars Rover over 34 million miles away to the surface of Mars. But even if life exists on Mars, it is unlikely they will ever find it. Do you know why? They will never find it, because of the Outer Space Treaty. Many nations agreed years ago that we would never knowingly contaminate another planet's biology with material from Earth. They know there's some frozen water there. The international community voted to avoid that area because if life is anywhere, it will be near water and they don't want to contaminate it. It's ironic to me that we will go 34 million miles away and go to such lengths to protect life on a microscopic level, but we won't offer that same protection to life in the womb.

It's our image of God that should cause us to value life. Regardless of skin color, or language, or culture—we value life. The Bible is the only book that teaches us that we are made in God's image. And really, what's the alternative if you don't believe that?

This is how Bertrand Russell summarizes it:
> "In the visible world, the Milky Way is a tiny fragment. Within this fragment, the solar system is an infinitesimal speck, and the speck —our planet is a microscopic dot. On this dot, tiny lumps of impure carbon and water complicated structure crawl about for a few years until they are dissolved again into the elements of which they are compounded." - Bertrand Russell, Atheist (11)

Isn't that depressing? Do you want that read at your funeral one day? Maybe he's right. Maybe we are all just cogs in the machine and it doesn't matter whether I love my kids or slug my kids. Nothing matters and nobody matters.

However, I know very few people, even those who believe in an impersonal beginning, who actually live that way. Genesis 1 says we are dominated by a world of personality and purpose, shot through with hope. As my Systematic Theology professor, Dr. James Leo Garrett, said, "God is both transcendent and immanent. He is all powerful, but at the same time, all loving."

You didn't come from somewhere, you came from Someone. And in this first chapter of Genesis, He envisioned you.

The question is? **How will you live out God's image in this world?**

Growing Roots Deeper

(Page numbers listed for answers may vary by one page.)

Chapter 1 Question for Bible Study

1. What ten words are the most quoted words in all of literature.? "__ ___ _____ ___ _____ ___ _____ ___ ___ _____." Genesis 1.1 (NIV) Page 2

2. God only had to _____. The Latin term used is *ex nihilo*—meaning, "___ __ _____." Page 2

3. _____ wasn't written as a science book, but as a love letter, or better yet a song written for us and about us. You must be careful about dissecting these passages as if it were a textbook. Page 5

4. Most cultures in Moses' day were polytheistic (belief in many gods). These gods were chaotic and _____. Therefore, life in these cultures was this constant exercise of trying to appease the gods. They had versions of a _____ _____. However, none of the other accounts of creation mention God's goodness and His _____. Page 4 & 5

5. Consider the difference in the pagan accounts, where humans are created as an _____ to relieve the gods of work. Contrasted by Genesis, where humanity is the very _____ __ _____. Page 5

6. God's first communication to them is a blessing that they are ____ __ _____ _____. Page 5

7. In Genesis 1:16-19, how could there be light because the sun doesn't show up until the fourth day? Again,

the point is more spiritual than scientific. Page 6

8. Who is the light of the world? Page 6

9. Is it possible to reconcile Genesis 1 with modern science? Think about pages 6-8 and record your answer.

10. Think about some of the quotes from great scientists on page 6-8. Was it all just from a speck? "In the beginning was a speck." Or was there a thoughtful plan?

11. Everyone matters to God because we were all made in His image. James 3:9 warns us not to curse people because ____ ___ ___ __ ____ _____. Page 9

12. God is all powerful, but at the same time, ___ _____." Page 10

13. How will you live out God's image in this world? Page 10

Footnotes for Chapter One

1. Celebrate Recovery is a biblical and balanced program that helps us overcome our hurts, hang-ups, and habits.
2. "graft" Encyclopædia Britannica. Encyclopædia Britannica Online. Encyclopædia Britannica Inc., 2016. Web. 25 Oct. 2016 <https://www.britannica.com/topic/graft>.
3. www.youtube.com/watch?v=J_hRRiXKdqc .
4. U.S. News & World Report, Dec. 23, 1991.
5. Patrick Glynn, "The Making and Unmaking of an Atheist," in: God: The Evidence (Rocklin,CA: Forum, 1997), 1—20.
6. Stephen Hawking, A Brief History of Time: From the Big Bang to Black Holes Paperback – (New York: Bantam, 1990), 156-157.
7. Quoted in Timothy Ferris, Coming of Age in the Milky Way, (New York, Morrow, 1988), 177.
8. The Los Angeles Times, Saturday 2nd May 1992.
9. Jastrow, R. 1978. God and the Astronomers. (New York, W.W. Norton), 116.
10. Quoted in Al Kresta, Dangers to the Faith: Recognizing Catholicism's 21st-Century Opponents. (Huntington, IN, Our Sunday Visitor), 1.
11. Bertrand Russell, "Dreams and Facts," The Athenaeum nos. 4,642, 4,623 (Apr 18, 25 1919), 198-9, 232-3 Repr. Chapter 2, Sceptical Essays (George Allen & Unwin, 1928)

CHAPTER 2
IT IS GOOD NOT TO BE ALONE

The creation story causes more controversy than even the life of Jesus. Therefore, many believers will at one time or another become engaged in debate or even arguments over the reliability of Genesis. I've discovered the more angry someone is when they debate Genesis, more often than not, it is their emotional issues masquerading as intellectual arguments.

Sometimes it's helpful to simply ask, "What is it about this topic that is making you so angry?" When you know the real issue behind the anger, it helps you to be more empathetic and, therefore, more helpful.

But what about the issues? Are Genesis 1 and 2 two separate, contradictory accounts? Or maybe it's the same story told in different ways.

Genesis 1 tells the story through the lens of the six days of creation, whereas, Genesis 2 tells a more thorough version of the 6th day.

Chapter 1 is a panorama of creation, and chapter 2 is the close-up. This was a very common way of writing for the Jewish people. It's called The Law of Recurrence. (12) The author will pause and give you more detail about something they've already written about. In this case, chapter 1 tells us God creates man and woman.

Chapter 2 tells us how He did that. Because this happened before the law and before the Fall, we see how things were intended to function in regards to work, rest, gender, and marriage. "The destiny of human creation is to live in God's world, with God's other creatures, on God's terms."- Dr. Walter Brueggemann, Old Testament Theologian (13)

Life's Sacred Rhythm

"Thus the heavens and the earth were completed in all their vast array. By the seventh day God had finished the work he had been doing; so on the seventh day he rested from all his work. And God blessed the seventh day and made it holy, because on that day he rested from all the work of creating. This is the account of the heavens and the earth when they were created, when the Lord God made the earth and the heavens." Genesis 2:1-4 (NIV)

A More Personal Look at God

In Genesis 1, the name given to God is Elohim. Elohim is not a name, but a title. It is used to describe deity. In Genesis 1, it occurs 35 times in 32 verses. Then in Genesis 2:4, there is a new phrase, Yahweh Elohim. In most of our English translations, it is "Lord, God." Elohim is a title, but Yahweh is a personal name. When you read "LORD" in the Old Testament, that is a placeholder. That is where the text says "Yahweh." The Jewish people never wanted to take Yahweh's name in vain, so they put in a substitute word there: Lord or Adonai in the Greek language. Elohim occurs some 2,600 times in the Old Testament. Yahweh occurs nearly 7,000 times.

What we can conclude is that God is personal. He has a name. Have you ever noticed how you feel when someone calls you by name? Don't you feel special or even loved? This is significant because Israel had been living for 400 years under Egyptian rule as slaves, and they had forgotten God's name. Moses, who wrote Genesis, wants the people to know it wasn't "Ra" the Egyptian god of the sun, but it was Yahweh who created the heavens and the earth.

That's why when God calls Moses, he says, "Who shall I tell them has sent me?" and God says, "Tell them 'I AM' is sending you."

The Dignifying of Human Labor and Rest

Genesis, chapter 2, describes what God did in creating the world as work. Therefore, we work just like God works. Remember, all the pagan accounts of creation described the work we do as relieving the gods of work that was beneath them. As believers, we are co-laborers with God. This is revolutionary!

Then God makes the seventh day and He rests. This is the sacred rhythm for human beings. God directs us not to work every day. Every seventh day, take a holiday or a holy day. God called every day good except the seventh day; He called it "holy."

If that is all we knew about the Sabbath, to rest like God, that would have been enough. The Sabbath law has been rescinded but the Sabbath principle has not because the Sabbath principle is tied to creation.
Does your work as well as your rest honor this principle?
What could you change to make it more honoring?

Creation Care

"Then the Lord God formed a man from the dust of the ground and breathed into his nostrils the breath of life, and the man became a living being." Genesis 2:7 (NIV)

"...so that they may rule over the fish in the sea and the birds in the sky, over the livestock and all the wild animals,[a] and over all the creatures that move along the ground." Genesis 1:26b (NIV)

This mandate is repeated in chapter 2: "The Lord God took the man and put him in the Garden of Eden to work it and take care of it." Genesis 2.15 (NIV)

We are God's stewards over the earth.

God's Provision in Eden

"Now the Lord God had planted a garden in the east, in Eden; and there he put the man he had formed." Genesis 2.8 (NIV)

What we discover here is that God, like an Italian wife who loves to cook, does not provide sparingly. Not only does He give us food, but it's good to look at, and it's delicious.

Sometimes people struggle with believing God is good. In Luke 11:11, Jesus said, when some people ask God for something, they think that He's going to give them what they didn't want at all. Like if we go to God for bread, that He will give a stone. Or like going to God for a fish, and He gives a snake. Just like Jesus taught, we know God isn't stingy. He is generous. We will see in the next chapter how sin messed up everything—everything except God. Sin didn't mess up God.

Creation Needs Our Management

By the way, you don't have to be an eco-nazi to care about the earth. When God announces His creation as "good," that word means inarguably perfect in every way. Humans have two jobs: to tend and to watch over. To tend is to cultivate. Adam has to encourage the garden to flourish and reach its potential. To watch over means to shepherd, which means to protect the animals from predators.

Why would we do this? We want to pass it on to the next generation.

In what ways do you care for creation for the next generation?

Gender Distinctions

"But for Adam, no suitable helper was found. So the Lord God caused the man to fall into a deep sleep; and while he was sleeping, he took one of the man's ribs and then closed up the place with flesh. Then the Lord God made a woman from the rib he had taken out of the man, and he brought her to the man." Genesis 2:20-22 (NIV)

The Significance of the "Helper"

When we read this from our cultural perspective, we sometimes misunderstand that God, in His Word, is demeaning women. When in fact, He is giving honor to women, which was unheard of in ancient days. Of the 19 times the word occurs in the Old Testament, 16 are in reference to God Himself – God is called the Helper. It doesn't mean second place, but it tells us how significant her contribution is. When God calls you a helper, He is saying, in this way, "You are like Me." When the Bible says she was fit for him (man), it means that she is the opposite of him. She is complementary to him. In the next chapter, we will discover how these desires to rule over one another is a result of the Fall.

The Unique Creation of Eve

Remember, Adam is not dreaming of a woman, "Five foot two, eyes of blue..." He doesn't know what he needs. Why doesn't God create Eve out of the dust of the ground like He did Adam?

First of all, it was God's plan, but also, Adam had to suffer something. He had to suffer a loss. God removed a living part of himself. He is no longer what he had been. He surrendered a part of himself for Eve to be made. He cannot be fully who he is until he's rejoined with what had been taken from him. This tells us something about marriage, doesn't it? Marriage is more than a union. It's a reunion. This is literally what the Bible means when it says "we become one flesh when we are united in marriage."

The First Recorded Human Words

"The man said, 'This is now bone of my bones and flesh of my flesh; she shall be called woman, for she was taken out of man.'" Genesis 2:23 (NIV)

The first recorded human words are poetry. The first three words literally mean, "This is it!" "The man perceives the woman not as his rival but as his partner, not as a threat because of her equality with himself, but as the only one capable of fulfilling his longing within."- Raymond C. Ortlund (14)

"Only the Hebrews, I mean only the Hebrews of all ancient peoples, made so much of their women, only they exploited their potential, their brains, and their courage. Only in the Bible, and I mean only in the Bible, do we find women often in the forefront of events." - Paul Johnson (15)

Marriage Instituted

The Four Essential Components of Marriage:

- Leaving – leave his parents. Many ancient and even present Middle-Eastern cultures believe that the parenting relationship was and is more sacred than marriage. The Bible says that this relationship, besides your relationship with God, becomes your most essential covenant in life.

- Cleaving – be united to his wife. This is a powerful word that means "glued together." It is used to

20

describe our relationship with God Himself. "Fear the Lord your God and serve him. Hold fast to him..." Deuteronomy 10:20 (NIV) This verse uses the same word translated as "cleave."

- Intimacy – to become one flesh. When Adam says, "Bone of my bone and flesh of my flesh," he is showing us that marriage is creating a new family. There is a permanency inherent in this statement.

- Transparency – naked and not ashamed. This means the barriers come down—you allow someone to know you deeply. In marriage, a part of that original transparency is regained. We recapture a little bit of Eden in marriage. Ultimately, what it means is they have complete faith and trust in one another. If faith and trust have been broken in your marriage, will you take every measure to restore it? I believe that faith and trust can be restored. Why would someone not want to take those steps? I believe, for some, it is difficult to be honest. To be honest means to be vulnerable. To be vulnerable means to be transparent. Transparency is also the answer to restoration. We must be honest with ourselves as well as our spouse.

The Sacred Romance

Genesis 2 rises in importance because our past is our future. Genesis 2 explains what happened before sin messed up the world. Today, we live in the present reality of a broken world. But what is yet to come, our future, reflects life for Adam and Eve before Genesis 2. God is at work to restore Eden. We all long for this reality. We long to be loved in this way—loved for who we are. It's what we mean when we pray, "Your Kingdom come, Your will be done."

"In all our hearts lies a longing for a Sacred Romance. It will not go away in spite of our efforts over the years to anesthetize or ignore its song...It's a Romance...set deeply within us..." - Brent Curtis and John Eldredge, The Sacred Romance: Drawing Closer to the Heart of God. (16)

Curtis and Eldredge are talking about this hunger for Eden. We sometimes get disappointed in relationships because we live in this sinful world, but remember, The Fall and sin did not change God.

This God who knows us best—loves us most. He knows all the things you like to hide; all the ways in which you pretend to have it together; and yet, His settled disposition towards you is love. He thought you were worth dying for.

When I invite that God into my life, I can be done with disappointments. That God never disappoints. He's always working for my good and my growth, and that's the God we serve. Now, I am not the man I used to be. And I'm still not the man I long to be, but God is working to take me back to Genesis 2.

Growing Roots Deeper

Chapter 2 Questions for Bible Study

1. Are Genesis 1 and 2 two separate, contradictory accounts? Or maybe it's the same story told in different ways. What do you think? Page 15

2. Genesis 1 tells the story through the lens of the six days of creation, whereas, Genesis 2 tells a more _____ _____ of the 6th day. Chapter 1 is a _____ of creation and chapter 2 is the _____. This was a very common way of writing for the Jewish people. Page 15

3. Chapter 2 tells us how He created and how things were intended to function in regards to ____< _____, _____, and _____. Pages 15-16

4. In Genesis 1, the name given to God is _____, not a name, but a title used to describe deity. In Genesis 2:4, there is a new phrase, Yahweh Elohim. In most of our English translations, it is "Lord, God." Elohim is a title, but Yahweh is a _____ _____. Elohim occurs

some 2,600 times in the Old Testament. Yahweh occurs nearly 7,000 times. If the Bible mentions God's name more than his title, what do you think it means to a believer? How does he want us to think of him? Page 16-17

5. God called every day good except the 7th day; He called it "holy." The Sabbath law has been rescinded but the Sabbath principle has not because the Sabbath principle is tied to creation. Does your work and your rest honor this principle? Page 17

6. What could you change to make it more honoring?

7. In what ways do you care for creation for the next generation?

8. When God calls the woman a helper, He is saying in this way she is like Him. When the Bible says she was fit for him (man). It means that she is the _____ of him. She is _____ to him. Page 19

9. Why doesn't God create Eve out of the dust of the ground like He did Adam? Page 19

10. Paul Johnson relates the fact that "only in the Bible do we find women often in the forefront of events." Does the world teach that fact? How can you help change that? Page 20

11. What are Four Essential Components of Marriage listed on pages 20-21?

12. In Genesis 2 God is at work to restore Eden. We all long to be _____ for who we are. It's what we mean when we pray, "Your Kingdom come, _____ ." Page 21

13. We sometimes get disappointed in relationships because we live in this sinful world, but remember, The Fall and sin did not change _____. This God who knows us best—loves us most. He knows all the things you like to hide; all the ways in which you pretend to have it together; and yet, He loves you. He thought you were _____. Page 22

14. Are you experiencing disappointments in a relationship? What can you do?

Footnotes for Chapter Two

12. James M. Gray, D.D., Synthetic Bible Studies or Thro' the Bible in a Year (Cleveland, OH, F.M. Barton, 1900), 15.
13. Walter Brueggemann. Interpretation Series (Louisville, KY, John Knox Press, 1986), 283.
14. Raymond C. Ortlund, Recovering Biblical Manhood and Womanhood, "Male-Female Equality and Male Headship," (Wheatland IL, Crossway, 1991), 101.
15. Paul Johnson, Heroes: Lessons for Today's Leaders, (New York, HarperCollins, 2007), 97.
16. Brent Curtis and John Eldredge, The Sacred Romance: Drawing Closer to the Heart of God, (New York, Thomas Nelson, 1997), 4.

CHAPTER 3
BROKEN

In the Fall of 2002, at the Metropolitan Museum of Art in New York City, a priceless, 15th-century marble statue of Adam, toppled over and shattered to pieces. No one was in the room. At first, they thought it was vandalism, but later they discovered a flaw in the pedestal. Even though it had never been done before, they attempted to restore Adam. Experts took the 28 recognizable pieces and the hundreds of unrecognizable pieces and tried to put them back together again. It was a modern-day Humpty Dumpty experiment. Finally, after twelve years and dozens of scientists and engineers, it was restored. The real story of Adam's restoration is what we will discover in this chapter.

Rick Warren told a story about preaching to 5,000 inmates. Most of the prisoners weren't listening, so he took out a $50 bill and asked who would like to have it. All hands went up. Then he crumpled it and then asked the same question. The inmates gave the same enthusiastic response. Then he spat on it and asked the question again. They, once again, all raised their hands. Then he stomped on it, asking again with the same hands raised. He said, "This is what has happened to you. Some of you have been used and abused. You've committed crimes you're paying for; sins you have struggled with. But you still haven't lost one cent of your value to God." (17)

That is what we see in Genesis 3.

The Fall - A Wedge Has Been Driven into Our Relationships

Now the serpent was more crafty than any of the wild animals the LORD God had made. He said to the woman, "Did God really say, 'You must not eat from any tree in the garden'?" 2 The woman said to the serpent, "We may eat fruit from the trees in the garden, 3 but God did say, 'You must not eat fruit from the tree that is in the middle of the garden, and you must not touch it, or you will die.'" 4 "You will not certainly die," the serpent said to the woman. 5 "For God knows that when you eat from it your eyes will be opened, and you will be like God, knowing good and evil." 6 When the woman saw that the fruit of the tree was good for food and pleasing to the eye, and also desirable for gaining wisdom, she took some and ate it. She also gave some to her husband, who was with her, and he ate it. Genesis 3:1-6 (NIV)

Why Two Trees?

One is called the Tree of Life. The other is the Tree of the Knowledge of Good and Evil and God says they cannot touch that one. The question is: if that tree is not good for us, why did God put it in the garden? Thomas Boston, a Scottish Puritan, said this is not just a test, it's a reminder that although Adam and Eve ruled over the entire world, we still have to submit to God. And happiness is only found in submission to Him. (18)

A Talking Snake?

The serpent was introduced without comment. There are lots of guesses out there: "Is it a fable?" I don't believe it's a fable. When the serpent spoke, you know something supernatural slithered on the scene. Moses' audience would've immediately understood that this snake was a mouthpiece for a dark power. Using the serpent was a subtle tactic of the Devil. The serpent is one of God's creatures. Adam and Eve have already been told they have dominion over all the earth and over all the creatures of the earth. That means that the serpent is below her and not above her, right? Therefore, she would not perceive it as being more powerful than her.

The temptation proved even more subtle by coming from below not above. It's unexpected and it's part of the Devil's strategy. Adam and Eve lived in a perfect environment, unscarred by hatred, violence, or sin. The nature of this temptation is not so much the forbidden fruit, but first and foremost to doubt God. The serpent suggests that they are being denied something by God that will make them happy.

The reason why we sin is we don't trust Him when He says, "This is not good for you. This will hurt you."

Satan suggested to Eve how unreasonable it was that God would restrict her happiness. By the way, this is a standard technique in an argument: to force an opponent to debate on your terms and place their position in the worst possible light.

Notice Satan doesn't use the personal name for God here. This is another ploy to convince Eve. In the last chapter, we read that God's personal name is Yahweh. We moved from the title of God, Elohim, in chapter 1, to

Yahweh Elohim, LORD God. When the serpent talked to Eve, he didn't use that title, but rather Elohim. Why would Satan do that? Satan subtly depersonalized Eve's relationship with God. If he began the debate with an assault on the character of God, Eve most likely would have shut him down right away. He simply sowed seeds of doubt in her mind, which is the way he has always worked.

The Vandalism of Shalom

Shalom means wholeness, completeness, fulfillment, and well-being. It describes peace with God, peace with others, and peace with ourselves. Shalom is the way things ought to be. Therefore, sin is the vandalism of shalom. There are three ways shalom gets vandalized:

- Our relationship with God is broken.

After they disobeyed, Adam and Eve did something they've never done before—they hide. This was just the beginning of human beings trying to hide from God.

- Our relationship with our closest friend is injured.

God questions Adam, "Who told you that you were naked? Have you eaten from the tree I told you not to eat from?"

Adam said, "Well, the woman you put here with me, gave me some of the fruit, and I ate it."

Think about it—Adam and Eve were the ones who had a perfect marriage up to this point. However, after this, they looked at one another in a totally different way. From this point on in relationship struggles, it would always be someone else's fault. Adam was almost suggesting, "I seem to recall it was your idea to give me this woman, God!"

• Our relationship with ourselves is disordered.

In order to blame you for my choices, what do I have to do first? I have to lie to myself. Somehow, what I have done has been caused by you. When this happens, you're no longer authentic, you begin to wear masks or fig leaves as it were.

> Dr. Timothy Keller in *The Reason for God* tells us, "We are told that as soon as we determined to serve ourselves instead of God, as soon as we abandoned living for and enjoying God as our highest good, the entire created world became broken. Human beings are so integral to the fabric of things that when human beings turned from God, the entire warp and woof of the world unraveled. Disease, genetic disorders, famine, natural disasters, aging, and death itself are as much the result of sin as are oppression, war, crime, and violence. We have lost God's shalom—physically, spiritually, socially, psychologically, culturally. Things now fall apart." - Dr. Timothy Keller, The Reason for God (19)

God's Amazing Response

"For as in Adam all die, so in Christ all will be made

alive." 1 Corinthians 15:22 (NIV)

The Bible tells us that Adam and Eve aren't just an illustration for us, but a representation of us. They are us. When we sin, we repeat their failure. We need to pay attention to how God responded to their failure because it is how He responds to you and me.

The surprise of the story is not the punishment, but His pursuit.

His Pursuit

Adam and Eve ran away from God, but God came looking for them. We have this tendency to think judgment comes first. But the Bible shows us over and over that what comes first is pursuit. They don't hear thunder booming, or judgment reigning down from heaven. The first thing they heard was the sound of God walking in the garden in the cool of the day. Does God know what's happened? Yes, He's God. But He acts as if nothing has changed, why? Because on His end, nothing has changed. This is why the Bible says, "When we are faithless, He remains faithful." 2 Timothy 2:13 (NIV) Our sin does not change God. But He knows it changes us.

His Prompting

"Then the Lord God called to Adam and said to him, 'Where are you?'" Genesis 3:9 (NKJV)

I love the questions of God in the Bible because we know an Omniscient Being never asks questions for information. He wants Adam to think about where he is.

"I heard You in the garden, and I was afraid because I

knew I was naked. I was filled with shame and I hid." Adam stumbles for a way to deal with these new feeling in 3:10.

This was the first mention of fear in the Bible. **Fear is always a consequence of sin.**

"Why have you eaten from the tree?" God asks in 3:11

Again, God knew the answer, He just wanted to see if Adam would be honest about it.

Summoning up all his courage in 3:12, Adam says, "It was the woman you gave me."

No one wants to face the truth about themselves. We always want to find a scapegoat. It is rare to hear someone say, "I just wanted what I wanted, and I didn't care who I hurt—I was bound and determined to get it." Do you think God was happy with Adam's answers? No, but even with Adam's less than stellar response, God still makes a promise.

His Promise

This is in Genesis 3:15. It's called the First Gospel. It's the first promise; the first prophecy. God forewarns us that there will be conflict.

Continual Conflict

"And I will put enmity between you and the woman, and between your offspring and hers." Genesis 3:15a

Enmity is hostility. One translation says, "This is going to be a war." This war won't just be between Eve and the Devil, but between her seed and the Devil's seed. This is unusual because the man carries the seed. Children are normally referred to as the seed of their father.

This wonderful prediction of the war to come is revealing. The seed of the woman refers to the One who would come as a result of the seed of the woman without the seed of the man. And who do we find out that is? Jesus! This is a prophecy of the virgin birth of Christ. This verse also points out that the seed of the woman will suffer temporary defeat.

Temporary Defeat

God again says to the serpent in the last part of 3:15: "...you will strike his heel."

Where does a snake usually bite somebody? Typically, it's below the knee right? This tells us two things: First, that sometimes Satan wins the battle. But also, when Christ died on the cross, Satan struck His heel. Again this prophecy literally comes true. When they nailed Jesus to the cross the nails went through His hands and His feet. The nails would be driven through the heels to hold the body in place.

Eventual Victory

"...he will crush your head..." is the middle of Genesis 3:15.

Most of us know that if you stomp on a snake's midsection, all you're going to do is make it mad. If you want to kill it, you have to crush its head. This verse says that even though the snake will bruise the heel of the seed of the woman, the seed of the woman would crush the serpent's head. What an amazing promise God gives us in response to the very first sin: God is a God who redeems.

His Provision

"The LORD God made garments of skin for Adam and his wife and clothed them." Genesis 3:21

Fig leaf clothing presents many problems. They fall apart easily. They itch. It's difficult to find the right size—but God steps in and provides. This is a foreshadowing as well. God's provision costs life: it involves sacrifice, blood, and death. Now we begin to see what it will take to ultimately cover our sin.

Farewell to Paradise

God's Measured Judgment
God is nothing like the pagan gods who are absolutely unpredictable in their wrath, anger, and judgment. When we say that God's judgment is arbitrary, we are projecting our woundedness on to God. We try to make God unfair and unjust. God's judgment is always made clear as to why it's done and how we can be free from it.

What is cursed and what is a consequence?
Verse 14 says the serpent is cursed. Verse 17 says the ground is cursed. Do you think human beings are cursed? What's the difference in a curse and a consequence? A curse is a pain or a loss that's directly or indirectly given by the lawgiver for the violation of the law. A consequence is a natural outcome of a transgression.

The ground is cursed: Man's dominion over the earth has been compromised. The ground will produce weeds, thorns, and even Brussels sprouts. But the man and the woman are not cursed. However, man and woman have to live with the consequences of sin. Verse 16 says that the woman's desire will be for her husband. This isn't a romantic word. It's a strong word in the Hebrew language that means she is going to desire her way. She is going to desire to control. And then the man also, as a result of sin, will seek to rule over her. The desire to have it your way is not just an old slogan from Burger King. That's sin!

The Bible continues to say the woman will suffer pain in childbirth. This too is a consequence, not a curse. The word used for pain in Hebrew does not mean physical pain. Old Testament scholar John Walton says this pain is psychological in nature. This is about the mental anguish that a woman endures as a mother. (20)

The Significance of Eve

"Adam named his wife Eve, because she would become the mother of all the living." Genesis 3:20 (NKJV)

Do you know what Eve means? Life. Remember the consequence of eating from the tree? Death. Why does Adam name her life? It is a reminder that he believes the promise of God: *One day the seed of that woman is going to rise up and crush that serpent's head.* Three truths we can take away from this story:

I can't go back.
I can't stay here.
I must go forward.

Adam could not go back and undo his sin. He would not be permitted to stay in paradise. Where did he go? East of Eden: since the Fall, we all live east of Eden. The only option he has left is to go forward.

The Tree is Guarded But It is Not Destroyed

What a great promise. John, the Apostle, would see that tree again:

"Then the angel showed me the river of the water of life, as clear as crystal, flowing from the throne of God and of the Lamb down the middle of the great street of the city. On each side of the river stood the tree of life, bearing twelve crops of fruit, yielding its fruit every month. And the leaves of the tree are for the healing of the nations." Revelation 22:1-2 (NIV)

We began in a garden and heaven takes us back to the garden. Where is the tree of life? At the throne of God! The leaves of that tree are about hope and healing. Jesus Christ opened the way to the very throne of God, the Holy of Holies.

Growing Roots Deeper

Chapter 3 Questions for Bible Study

1. In the Garden of Eden, there were two trees. One is called the Tree of Life and the other is the Tree of the Knowledge of Good and Evil. God says they cannot touch the Tree of the Knowledge of Good and Evil. The question is why. If that tree is not good for us, why did God put it in the garden? Page 28

2. Do you think the serpent was real, a fable or does it matter to you? Page 29

3. Moses' audience would've immediately understood that this snake was a mouthpiece for a _____ _____. Page 29

4. Adam and Eve lived in a perfect environment, unscarred by hatred, violence, or sin. The nature of this temptation is not so much the forbidden fruit, but first and foremost to _____ _____. Page 29

5. The serpent suggests that they are _____ _____ _____ by God that will _____ _____ _____. Page 29

6. Satan suggested to Eve how unreasonable it was that God would _____ _____ _____. Page 29

7. Satan subtly _____ Eve's relationship with God. He simply sowed seeds of doubt in her mind which is the way he has always worked. Page 30

8. After they disobeyed, Adam and Eve did something they've never done before—they _____. Page 30

9. When God questioned Adam, "Who told you that you were naked? Have you eaten from the tree I told you not to eat from?" What did Adam do? Page 30

10. From this point on in relationship struggles, it would always be someone else's _____. In order to blame you for my choices, what do I have to do first? Pages 30-31

11. Corinthians 15:22 "For as in Adam all _____, so in Christ, all will be made alive." Page 31&32

12. The Bible tells us that Adam and Eve aren't just an illustration for us, but a _____ of us. They are __ . When we ____ , we repeat their failure. Page 32

13. Adam and Eve ran away from God, but God ____
_____ ___ _____ . Page 32

14. This was the first mention of fear in the Bible. Fear is always a consequence of ____. Page 33

15. "And I will put enmity between you and the woman, and between your offspring and hers. Genesis" 3:15a. Who is God talking to in this passage? Who is the woman's offspring?   Page 33

16. This is a prophecy of the virgin birth of Christ and points out that the ____ __ _____ will suffer temporary defeat. Page 34

17. Christ died on the cross, Satan struck His heel. Again this prophecy literally comes true. When they nailed Jesus to the cross the nails went through His hands and His feet. The nails would be driven through the heels to hold the body in place. When you read this paragraph, what did you know without a doubt? Page 34

18. What is the amazing promise God gives us in response to the very first sin: ____ ___ __ ____ _____ _____ . Page 35

19. We try to make God unfair and unjust. God's
_____ is always made clear on why it's done
and how we can be free from it. A consequence is a
natural outcome of a _____. Page 35

20. What does the name Eve mean? Page 36

21. Where in the Gospel do we see this tree again?
Page37

22. Where is the tree of life? Page 37

23. The leaves of that tree are about _____ and
_____. Page 37

24. When did you first realize God died for you? How did
you respond to that sacrifice?

Footnotes for Chapter Three

17. www.preachingtoday.com/illustrations/2014/september.
18. Boston, Thomas. A View of the Covenant of Grace. Introduction by Malcolm H. Watts. (Choteau, MT, Old Paths Gospel Press, 1990) 34.
19. Timothy Keller, The Reason for God: Belief in the Age of Skepticism. (New York, Penguin Group, 2008), 170.
20. John H. Walton, The NIV Application Commentary: Genesis. (61) (Grand Rapids, MI, Zondervan), 219.

CHAPTER 4
EAST OF EDEN

Living East of Eden has become a metaphor: "The farther East you are from Eden, the farther you are away from God." Genesis 4 shows us how sin begins to spread like a virus. It infects and it affects everything and everybody.

This chapter introduces another common theme—the difficulty brothers have getting along—Cain and Abel, Isaac and Ishmael, Jacob and Esau, Joseph and his brothers. However, this story is more than just sibling rivalry. Genesis 4 is also the story of many firsts: the first birth, brothers, shepherd, farmer, offerings, worship service, murder, and a cover-up.

The Generation After Eden

"Adam made love to his wife Eve, and she became pregnant and gave birth to Cain. She said, 'With the help of the Lord I have brought forth a man.'" Genesis 4:1 (NIV)

When Eve says, "With the help of the Lord," it means more than the Lord gave her a child. She is most likely referencing the promise from Genesis 3:15. The promise was that one day, through her seed, One would rise up and crush the serpent's head. And she may have thought, "Maybe this is the One." Eve has no idea of the time from promise to fulfillment. Well, it didn't take her long to realize the one born to her was not a savior, but a trouble-maker. He was not part of the solution—he was part of the problem. When Abel is born, she isn't nearly as optimistic. The Hebrew word for Abel is ha'bel, which means "fleeting" or a "vapor." It's a statement about how fragile life can be.

In the course of time, Cain brought some of the fruits of the soil as an offering to the Lord. And Abel also brought an offering—fat portions from some of the firstborn of his flock. The Lord looked with favor on Abel and his offering, but on Cain and his offering, he did not look with favor. So Cain was very angry, and his face was downcast. Genesis 4:3-5 (NIV)

Both brought the Lord an offering, but Cain's offering was rejected. Why? What was the difference? This takes place long before God gives the law, where God tells them specifically what offerings are acceptable. How did they know how to give an offering? They knew because God showed them in chapter 3. Do you remember how God clothed them? God killed two animals to make a covering for their shame. To cover sin, you need a sacrifice of blood. Abel believed and understood this.

"By faith Abel brought God a better offering than Cain did." Hebrews 11:4 (NIV)

Abel's offering proved better because it lined up with the way God showed him, and also because it was by faith. Faith isn't just a belief in anything. The Bible says in Romans 10:17, "faith comes by hearing and hearing by the Word of God." Faith believes in what God has said and what God had done.

We come to God in the way He shows us to come to Him. It is a common belief that people can come to God in any way they want as long as they are sincere. Yet, if you believe the Bible is God's Word, He tells us exactly how to come to Him.

That was Quick

From eating the forbidden fruit, things escalate quickly. Cain commits murder. Sin has infected and affected all.

God Pleads with Cain

"So Cain was very angry, and his face was downcast. Then the Lord said to Cain, 'Why are you angry? Why is your face downcast? If you do what is right, will you not be accepted? But if you do not do what is right, sin is crouching at your door; it desires to have you, but you must rule over it.'" Genesis 4:5-7 (NIV)

Back in chapter 3, we were introduced to two results of sin—fear and shame. Now, in chapter 4 we are introduced to another—anger. God is showing Cain, that if you nurse a grudge; if you hang on to resentment, then the door is wide open to the Enemy. Do you know what the Enemy does with that? He tempts you to go farther than you ever meant to go.

God warned him, "Sin is crouching at your door." Sin is predatory. Watch out for temptation to nurse a wounded spirit.

A Murder Even God Could Not Stop

"Now Cain said to his brother Abel, 'Let's go out to the field." While they were in the field, Cain attacked his brother Abel and killed him." Genesis 4:8 (NIV)

The key word is repeated seven times in eleven verses:

"brother." The issues between those we love can cut the deepest. This did escalate so quickly. It didn't occur after years of violence. In the last chapter the serpent had to talk Eve into sin; now God can't talk Cain out of it. Yet again, we learn this important principle.

Sin Doesn't Change God

"Then the Lord said to Cain, 'Where is your brother Abel?' 'I don't know,' he replied. 'Am I my brother's keeper?'" Genesis 4:9 (NIV)

God questioned Cain just as He did Cain's father, Adam. With this question, God gave him a chance to confess. But Cain, like his father, tried to hide what he'd done. This is another example of The Law of Recurrence. Chapter 4 is a retelling of chapter 3.

In both stories:
- They disobey.
- God sought them out.
- God questioned them.
- They were banished from where they lived and the ground became cursed.

Yet in both chapters, God showed mercy. Sin ruined everything but it did not change God. However, it does change us. Because sin changes our view of God, we need this reminder. We need the reminder so that we might have hope when we are struggling.

Cain is Less than Honest

Remember, when God asked this question, He wasn't seeking information, but a confession. When God questioned Adam, Adam's answers were filled with blame. In this case, Cain just tells a bold-faced lie. In asking if he is his brother's keeper, he is denying what we are really supposed to be about—looking out for one another. Yes, you are your brother's keeper.

The Blood Cries Out

"The Lord said, 'What have you done? Listen! Your brother's blood cries out to me from the ground. Now you are under a curse and driven from the ground, which opened its mouth to receive your brother's blood from your hand. When you work the ground, it will no longer yield its crops for you. You will be a restless wanderer on the earth.'" Genesis 4:10-12 (NIV)

The Hebrew word for blood is plural which always means blood that was shed in violence. The word for cry in Hebrew is tsa'aq and is used for human expressions of the most desperate, extreme need. "The rivers of your brother's blood cries desperately to be avenged." In other words, this kind of activity requires God's response. God always hears desperate cries.

How Does Cain Respond?

"Cain said to the Lord, 'My punishment is more than I can bear.'" Genesis 4:13 (NIV)

Even though this really was a merciful punishment, he was still only concerned with himself. First of all, he feared someone would try to kill him. Ironically, he's worried that someone might do to him, what he did to Abel. This is another reiteration of reaping and sowing. God, however, promised Cain extra protection. He marked Cain in such a way that people would instantly know that he was different and under the protection of God.

People have asked me over the years, "What is that mark?" And with full confidence and years of theological training, I say, "I have no idea!" In the Torah, this word is used to describe the stars as signs. It's used as the signs or miracles before Pharaoh.

But we do know this: it kept Cain safe. That's God's mercy. Grace is when we receive something good we don't deserve. Mercy is when we don't receive something bad we do deserve. If this story teaches us anything, it teaches us that there is nothing that can separate us from the love of God. However, there are consequences. We see this in Cain's lineage.

A Society Without God

Cain moves to the land of Nod, which in Hebrew means wandering. While the consequences would become obvious, we can also see some things Cain accomplishes:

Construction (v. 17-18)

Cain built a city, he built a family, and he built a legacy. He was the first city planner and the first real estate developer.

At this point, you may have the nagging question that many people want to know. Where did Cain get his wife? He must've married a sister, niece, or grand-niece. In the beginning, this was not against the law. Also, people lived hundreds of years back then. Genesis 5.5 says Adam lived 930 years. Let's say they only had children the first 500 years spaced out every 5 years. That's 100 children! Another viewpoint is given by scholar, James Montgomery Boice, who said if half the normal number of children grew up and half of those got married and half of those had children, Adam could have seen 1 million descendants in his lifetime. (21)

Corruption (v.19)

"Lamech (Cain's son) married two women, one named Adah and the other Zillah." Genesis 4:19 (NIV)

Sin is escalating. First, the sanctity of life has been desecrated and now, the sanctity of marriage. Remember in Genesis 2, God set the ordinance of marriage being between one man and one woman for life. There are many examples of polygamy in the Old Testament and typically the writers don't comment on it, but you can read for yourself the consequences. This is the nature of narrative writing. What you will quickly discover is that it never ends well. It degrades women, and it goes against God's created order.

Culture (vv. 20-22)

You would think that Moses, the writer, would have nothing good to say about Cain and his descendants, but that's not true. Even sinful human beings can create some pretty amazing things. They had a bluegrass band and even made tools!

We are all made in the image of God. This is another great apologetic—the objectivity of beauty. God gives us beauty to show us His love. Beauty is not primarily functional, but simply for our enjoyment.

This was another powerful principle I learned from my philosophy class at Southwestern Seminary. Dr. Yandall Woodfin was my professor and wrote about this in his book:

With All Your Mind: A Christian Philosophy. He writes, "A responsibility is, therefore, laid on men collectively and, as far as it is conceivable, universally, to discern and acknowledge beauty as the creative ground and structural basis for the symmetry, brilliance, and purity of being which become tangible in beautiful forms. In its highest manifestations, beauty often reflects a numinous quality closely akin to that which men experience religiously as "the holy." (22)

Crime (vv.23-24)

"Lamech said to his wives, 'Adah and Zillah, listen to me; wives of Lamech, hear my words. I have killed a man for wounding me, a young man for injuring me. If Cain is avenged seven times, then Lamech seventy-seven times.'" Genesis 4:23-24 (NIV)

This is the oldest recorded song in the Bible. And possibly the first "gangsta rap." He really was a thug. He boasted about getting away with murder.

The Progress of Sin

The serpent talked Eve into sin.
Adam sinned on his own.
God couldn't talk Cain out of sin.
Lamech was bragging about his sins.

Along with music, art, industry, you also have polygamy, murder, and violence. Despite the consequences of sin, God was still showing mankind his grace and providence.

What Does this Mean for Us? - Living in a Violent Society

Not only do human beings behave badly, but we've grown accustomed to it. School shootings, acts of terror, abortion clinics, we can't keep up with what is going on each week. Remember in Luke 9:54 when the brothers came to Jesus because the Samaritans were inhospitable to them, and they asked Jesus if they should call down fire from heaven to consume them? Jesus rebuked them and said that is not His way. John, who was part of the committee calling for fire to rain down on the Samaritans, eventually learned Jesus' way:

"For this is the message which you heard from the beginning, that we should love one another, and not be like Cain who was of the evil one and murdered his brother. And why did he murder him? Because his own deeds were evil and his brother's righteous. Do not wonder, brethren, that the world hates you." 1 John 3:11-13a (RSV)

John learned that both love and hate originate outside of us. John wrote in 1 John 4:19 we love because He first loved us. Hate comes from the Enemy. If you struggle with hate, you have the same struggle Cain had. And he was in the grip of the Devil. God looks at the heart. He doesn't have to wait for the action.

"You have heard that it was said to the men of old, 'You shall not kill; and whoever kills shall be liable to judgment.' But I say to you that every one who is angry with his brother shall be liable to judgment; whoever insults his brother shall be liable to the council, and whoever says, 'You fool!' shall be liable to the hell of fire." Matthew 5:21-22 (RSV)

Believer, it doesn't mean you cease to be a Christian when

you hate, it means you cease to act like one. We must have high hopes for humanity, but low expectations. Our hope comes from the Good News of the Gospel. Yet we understand what Jesus taught us when He said, "The road is narrow that leads to life." (23)

The World isn't Getting Worse
Our Information is Getting Better

Ray Kurzweil an inventor and a futurist works for Google. He said, "On the effect of the modern information era: People think the world's getting worse, and we see that on the left and the right, and we see that in other countries. People think the world is getting worse...That's the perception. What's actually happening is our information about what's wrong in the world is getting better. A century ago, there would be a battle that wiped out the next village, and you'd never even hear about it. Now there's an incident halfway around the globe, and we not only hear about it, we experience it." - Ray Kurzweil, Postback Conference (24)

Be careful about the good-old-days syndrome. Do you remember the near-perfect little town called Mayberry from The Andy Griffith Show? Mayberry never was.

Why Biblical Violence is Good for Your Kids

No human activity is mentioned more in the Old Testament than violence. This reminds us that the Bible is about real people. It doesn't read like a fairy tale.

The Old Testament books "...contain over six hundred passages that explicitly talk about nations, kings, or individuals attacking, destroying, and killing others...No other human activity or experience is mentioned as often." - Raymund Schwager (25)

Our kids are exposed to violence all the time. The difference is that in our society it tends to be glorified, and there aren't always consequences. The problem isn't that there's violence in the Bible. If there wasn't, we would think it was a fairy tale. The problem is how we interpret that violence. The Bible is a "text in travail." When some people describe violence, they sometimes try to hide the voice of the victim. But in the Bible, we are forced to listen to the unheard victim. The Bible is one of the only books in history that tells both sides of the story.

Therefore, it's good for your children, when they are old enough to understand, to hear these stories because there will always be a critique of that violence.

Many people deal with violence at its tipping point, not at its source. It's not the means that matter as much as the motive. The greatest weapon of mass destruction is the human heart. Jesus taught us the heart of the matter in the Sermon on the Mount.

"You have heard that it was said to the people long ago, 'Do not murder, and anyone who murders will be subject to judgment.' But I tell you that anyone who is angry with his brother will be subject to judgment." Matthew 5:21-22 (NIV)

You can't talk about school shootings without talking about rage. You can't talk about terrorism without talking about hate.

"Again Jesus called the crowd to him and said, 'Listen to me, everyone, and understand this. Nothing outside a person can defile them by going into them. Rather, it is what comes out of a person that defiles them... For it is from within, out of a person's heart, that evil thoughts come—sexual immorality, theft, murder, adultery, greed, malice, deceit, lewdness, envy, slander, arrogance and folly. All these evils come from inside and defile a person.'" Mark 7:14-23 (NIV)

Adultery is not primarily caused by someone's good looks. Greed is not primarily caused by money. And envy is not primarily caused by the lottery. And violence is not primarily caused by video games and movies. I'm not saying that external stimuli don't have an effect on people, but the instinct, the choice to act out, always originates in the heart.

"The followers of Jesus have been called to peace. When he called them they found their peace, for he is their peace.... they are told that they must not only have peace but make it. And to that end they renounce all violence."- Dietrich Bonhoeffer (26)

What Bonhoeffer was saying is that we don't need vigilantes, we need vigilance. We need to live in God's perfect shalom. Satan has vandalized shalom, but as Christ followers, we can take it back. What you say matters. What you do matters.

Does it contribute to the problem or does it contribute to the solution? Does your Gospel step into the difficult situations of life and bring hope and healing?

Growing Roots Deeper

Chapter 4 Questions for Bible Study

1. Living East of Eden has become a metaphor: "The farther East you are from Eden, the farther you are _____ _____ ____." Page Page 43

2. When was a time in your life when you felt you were living East of Eden?

3. "With the help of the Lord" means more than the Lord gave Eve a child. It most likely means the promise from Genesis 3:15. The promise was that one day, through her seed, One would rise up and _____ ____ _____ ____. Pages 43

4. What does Abel mean in the Hebrew language? Page 44

5. Abel also brought an offering of the ___ _____ from some of the firstborn of his flock. Cain brought

some of the _____ __ ___ _____ as an offering to the Lord. Cain's offering was rejected. Why? What was the difference? Page 44

6. God is showing Cain, that if you nurse a _____; if you hang on to _____, then the door is wide open to the Enemy. What does the Enemy do with that? Page 45

7. In Genesis 4 a keyword is repeated 7 times in 11 verses. What is the word? Page 45 & 46

8. What is the important principle we learn in seeing Cain's sin and his reaction to God? Page 47

9. Although we don't know what the Mark of Cain was, what did it do? Page 48

10. There are many examples of polygamy in the Old Testament and typically the writers don't comment on it, but what does page 49 list as one of the consequences?

11. What does Jesus say about how to respond to a violent society? Page 51

12. 1 John 4:19 says we love because He _____ _____ __ . Hate comes from the _____. Page 51

13. Do you agree that Biblical violence is good for kids? What can you do to help young people stand strong and hopeful? Pages 52 & 53

14. Bonhoeffer says, "We don't need _____, we need _____." What you say matters. What you do matters. Does it contribute to the _____ or does it contribute to the _____? Page 54

15. Ask yourself, does my Gospel step into the difficult situations of life and bring hope and healing?

Footnotes for Chapter Four

21. James Montgomery Boice, Genesis: An Expositional Commentary (Ada, MI, Baker Books, 1982) 368.
22. #Yandall Woodfin, With All Your Mind: A Christian Philosophy. (Fort Worth, TX, Scripta Publishing, 1980), 116-117
23. Matthew 7:14
24. Quoted by Todd Bishop, www.geekwire.com, July 2016
25. Raymund Schwager, Must There Be Scapegoats? Violence and Redemption in the Bible, (Stanford, CA, Stanford University Press, 1987), 47
26. #Dietrich Bonhoeffer, The Cost of Discipleship, (New York: Macmillan, 1966) 123

CHAPTER 5
A RADICAL GOD

Chapter 5 is a genealogy—so let's just confess to one another: when you come to the "begats" in your Bible reading, do you ever skip ahead? Even if that is true more often than not, we must acknowledge the importance of genealogies in Scripture.

The new idea in science is the theory of everything. They are looking for one theory to tie all the other theories together, a unified explanation. What they will figure out one day is—we really do have the explanation already in the book of Genesis.

The theme we find in the first few pages, we find in the last few pages of the Bible as well. And because we are in between the beginning and the end, our goal in applying this chapter is to get radical.

We usually think of radical as extreme—but it literally means to get back to your roots. Therefore, you are radical if you can connect back to your beginning. You are radical when you get back to what life was meant to be for you. This is why we believe that your story began before you were born. And Genesis 5 is about our roots—where we came from.

"This is the written account of Adam's family line. When God created mankind, he made them in the likeness of God. He created them male and female and blessed them. And he named them "Mankind" when they were created. When Adam had lived 130 years, he had a son in his own likeness, in his own image; and he named him Seth. After Seth was born, Adam lived 800 years and had other sons and daughters. Altogether, Adam lived a total of 930 years, and then he died." Genesis 5:1-5 (NIV)

We can better understand the importance of genealogies by highlighting four core truths:

The Line of Cain Versus the Line of Seth

This lineage covers the creation to the Flood and although humanity is getting further away from God, you have ten families that stood for the Lord:

Adam 930 years
Seth 912 years
Enosh 905 years
Kenan 910 years
Mahalalel 895 years
Jared 962 years
Enoch 365 years
Methuseleh 969 years
Lamech 777 years

The first thing you can't help but notice is the life spans of these men. Because of these long life spans, it makes people wonder, "Is this for real?" The only explanation is the conditions on earth before the flood were radically different after the flood.

Did you notice Cain is not mentioned? Because of the

murder and Cain moving away, his line is not relevant. Genesis 5 traces the line of faith which is why Cain is not mentioned. His lineage is a cul-de-sac: it begins with Cain and ends with Lamech, the wicked son who commits murder and brags about it. He even says God won't do anything about it. The branch of that family tree gets pruned away because of their own choices.

The difference in Seth and Cain are more than just about brothers. They represent two different trajectories in life: one is characterized by unbelief and rebellion against God. The other is characterized by faith and following God. Chapter 4 and chapter 5 are really opposites: one about the self-loving Cain, and the other about the God-loving Seth. With Seth, there's no great achievement mentioned like with Cain. But they are distinguished by this phrase: "They walked with God."

Cain built for his sons, but Seth built into his sons. Cain sacrificed his family for success, but Seth believed that success is building his family. You can't help but notice the differences in the two. Not only that, the cemetery is filling up East of Eden.

After the flood, life expectancy drops by 50%, by the time we get to the Tower of Babel which is chapter 11, it drops by another 50%, then we read in Psalms the life expectancy is 70-80 years. But there's something more to this chapter. We see this in the next truth:

The Reversal of the Law of Primogeniture

The Book of Genesis is very concerned with the progress of the seed of the woman. The seed of the woman will one day rise up and crush the serpent's head. Genesis is recording who is the seed and who is not the seed. It's not Cain. It's

Seth, the third born. It's not Japeth and Ham, it's Shem, the third born. It's not Ishmael, it's Isaac. It's not Esau, it's Jacob. Genesis is recording Messianic history. And what we discover is that the seed is never who you might expect it to be.

In Middle-Eastern culture, if you were to ask who will be the favored son, it would always be the eldest. The law of primogeniture demands that the eldest is the one who carries the family identity forward. This law is so sacred a principle in the ancient world that it is never violated. With God, however, it's not birth order that determines who's in and who's out.

Primogeniture meant that the big brother always gets more – more respect, more status, more prestige, more of everything, including and most importantly, most if not all of the family's assets. In those days, if you were not the first born, you were on the outside and on the downside. This is where feudalism comes from. In the same way, the first-born son received all the land, in feudalism, if you weren't born royal, you could never have land and you were a serf or a servant forever. The problem of primogeniture, which led to feudalism, is what, in part, led to the founding of this country.

John Locke, who was a major influence on our founding fathers and the Constitution, stood up against the kings and lords. Do you know what guided his thinking? The Bible. It was translated into English for the first time, and he was able to read the Genesis story.

"...one of the most important narrative threads in Genesis is 'the reversal of the iron law of primogeniture.'" – Robert Alter, Professor of Hebrew and Comparative Literature at the University of California, Berkeley (27)

Since then, God always chooses the most unlikely person to carry out His plan. How unlikely are you to be chosen by God to carry out His plan?

THE MAN WHO WALKED WITH GOD

"Enoch walked faithfully with God 300 years and had other sons and daughters. Altogether, Enoch lived a total of 365 years. Enoch walked faithfully with God; then he was no more, because God took him away." Genesis 5:22b-24 (NIV)

Enoch has the shortest life span in Genesis 5. This is the briefest biography of anyone in the Bible, and yet he's mentioned in the New Testament three different times.

"By faith Enoch was taken from this life, so that he did not experience death: 'He could not be found, because God had taken him away.' For before he was taken, he was commended as one who pleased God." Hebrews 11:5 (NIV)

Don't you want to be one who pleases God? Although there were many people in Scripture who pleased God, it is only said of two people—Enoch and Jesus. And that phrase, "walked with God," is only used to describe a few people— Adam and Eve, Enoch, Noah, and Abraham. Also, Enoch was only one of two who never dies. The other was Elijah.

In a sense, Enoch recovered what Adam and Eve lost. Remember they walked with God in the cool of the day? And when they sinned they were rejected from the garden and ceased to walk with God. But now Enoch is able to walk with God. This is what it means when the Bible says "pray without ceasing" in 1 Thessalonians 5. It's more than just a quiet time, but a continual relationship. Also, consider this: Enoch walked with God outside of Paradise. Adam and Eve walked with God in Paradise. That's what made Paradise, paradise

—that God was there walking with them. In other words, Enoch figured out how to walk with God in a broken, messed up world. This word for walked, *halakh,* is intensive in its voice, so it means he really enjoyed this walk. This was his source of joy! From the beginning of time, all that God has ever wanted was a walking partner:

1. It's what God created us to do.
2. It's what Adam forfeited.
3. It's what God still requires.
4. It's what Christ makes possible.

"He has shown you, O man, what is good; And what does the Lord require of you but to do justly, to love [a]mercy, and to walk humbly with your God?" Micah 6:8 (NKJV)

Jesus removed the barrier that we put between us and God —sin. And by Enoch not dying, we learn one of the most powerful truths in Genesis: We weren't born to die, we were born to live. And the life we crave comes from walking with God. Look at how important walking with God is.

"I'll set up my residence in your neighborhood; I won't avoid or shun you; I'll stroll through your streets. I'll be your God; you'll be my people." Leviticus 26:11-12 (The Message)

At the end of the book of Revelation, Christ is walking among the seven candlesticks. What do they represent? The churches. God's people are always walking with God, which also means they are a people on the move. The first dwelling place of God was a Tabernacle. The ark of the covenant was made to be moved. The Passover was to be eaten in a hurry... "with their shoes on and their walking stick in hand," to remind them that they are a people on the move. You have to be ready to go wherever the Spirit may lead you.

The Christian life is described as a walk. We're told to walk in newness of life (Romans 6:4), walk by faith (2 Corinthians 57), walk worthy of our vocation (Ephesians 4:1), walk circumspectly (Ephesians 5:15), walk honestly (1 Thessalonians 4:12), walk worthy of the Lord (Colossians 1:10), walk in light (1 John 1:7), walk in the truth (3 John 4), walk in the Spirit (Galatians 5:16), and walk in love (Ephesians 5:2).

We walk with God as we go on the mission and as a matter of communion. And because of the Gospel, we are able to be on mission and commune with Him. The Gospel is possible because of this next principle.

THE GOD WHO IS SLOW TO ANGER AND JUDGMENT

Enoch named his son Methuselah. Methuselah's name literally means, "His death shall bring it," or loosely translated, "When he dies, it will come." We also learn in the book of Jude (1:14) in the New Testament, that Enoch was given a revelation from God about the future and it didn't look good because judgment was coming. And he was told to give his son this name. His son, became a walking, breathing sermon illustration. "When he dies, it will come." What will come? The judgment. We know Methuselah lived to be 969 years old. The year he died, the Flood came. But many people miss that because he lived so long, it says so much about the mercy of God. God delays judgment. It's as if God is saying, "You are destroying each other, you are living in disobedience, and I won't allow it. By the way, I'm going to give you almost 1000 years to repent."

Enoch knew, "As long as my son is living, God is holding back judgment." Why does God delay? He would rather bring rescue instead of judgment. Can you imagine raising a child like that? Every time he'd get a cold, the whole neighborhood would just gasp. Everybody's bringing him chicken soup... "Is he better?" But really and truly, our God would rather give mercy.

"The Lord will rise up as he did at Mount Perazim, he will rouse himself as in the Valley of Gibeon—to do his work, his strange work, and perform his task, his alien task." Isaiah 28:21 (NIV)

God's judgment is described as alien and strange to God. You can mark it down, God is not unpredictable—He never flies off the handle. He doesn't arbitrarily devastate people with tornadoes or hurricanes. Even His judgment is tempered by mercy. Even when His people lie to His face. Here's how it was back then:

"Now the earth was corrupt in God's sight and was full of violence." Genesis 6:11 (NIV)

Satan has vandalized shalom. We have lost our critique of violence even today.

But if you read Genesis, your critique can be restored. We can understand how much violence does damage to the people made in the *imageo Dei*. No one would consider God a just God if He ignored the corruption and the violence in this world. This is why Hell makes sense to me—justice is never fully served in this life. Those who escape justice in this life are brought to justice. God will judge the world just like He did in Noah's day, but His preference is mercy.

"Say to them, 'As I live,' declares the Lord God, 'I take no pleasure in the death of the wicked, but rather that the wicked turn from his way and live. Turn back, turn back from your evil ways! Why then will you die, O house of Israel?'" Exodus 33:11 (NIV)

"The Lord is not slow in keeping his promise, as some understand slowness. He is patient with you, not wanting anyone to perish, but everyone to come to repentance." 2 Peter 3:9 (NIV)

Peter is saying that God is so slow in bringing judgment that some people accuse God of dragging His feet. The God of the Bible is not angry in the Old Testament, but then has a change of heart and becomes kinder and gentler in the New Testament. This is the God of the Bible:

"...You are a gracious and compassionate God, slow to anger and abounding in love, a God Who relents from sending calamity..." Jonah 4:2 (NIV)

These words are so important that they're quoted verbatim throughout the rest of the Old Testament. In Exodus 34:6-7; Numbers 14:18; Nehemiah 9:17; Psalm 103:8,17; 145:8; Jeremiah 32:18-19; Joel 2:13; and Jonah 4:2. You can also hear echoes of it in Deuteronomy 5:9-10; 1 Kings 3:6; Lamentations 3:32; Daniel 9:4; and Nahum 1:3. This is one of the most foundational statements about God, yet one of the most neglected.

"Compassionate" is from the Hebrew *raham*, which is the same root as the word for "womb." God feels about you the way a mother feels about her child in the womb.

"Gracious" (Hebrew word *chanan*.) The root means "to bend, to be inclined." This describes God bending toward us in our weakness.

"Slow to Anger" – In other words, God is patient. 1 Corinthians 13 describes love perfectly—God IS love. This loving God is in no hurry to judge sinners.

"Loving-kindness" This is the Hebrew word, *chesed*. This is the same word as we find in the New Testament, translated as "grace." God abounds in grace, doesn't He?

Some people have trouble reconciling this Grace with God's judgment. Here are four things about God's judgment by Norm Geisler:

1. It's always announced in advance by God's prophets. "This is coming. It's coming from Me. And this is why."
2. It's always for a specific act of rebellion against God.
3. There is always a period of time given for repentance.
4. There is always a way of escape. (28)

Let's get radical! In other words, let's get back to our roots and understand who God is. When people really understand who God is, they run into His arms. Get back to what you were made to do—walk with God.

Growing Roots Deeper

Chapter 5 Questions for Bible Study

1. When you come to the "begats" in your Bible reading, do you ever skip ahead?   Be honest. We must acknowledge the importance of _____ in Scripture. Page 59

2. The theme we find in the first few pages, we find in the last few pages of the Bible as well. And because we are in between the beginning and the end, our goal in applying this chapter is to ___ _____ . Page 59

3. How long did Adam live? Page 60

4. Notice in the lineage of Adam, Seth is mentioned. Why is Cain not mentioned? Page 60-61

5. Chapter 4 and chapter 5 of Genesis are really opposites: one about the ____-_____ ____, and the other about the ____-_____ ____. Pages 61

6. Cain sacrificed his _____ for success, but Seth believed that success is building his _____. Page 61

7. _____ meant that the big brother always gets more – more respect, more status, more prestige, more of everything, including and most importantly, most if not all of the family's assets. Page 62

8. John Locke, who was a major influence on our founding fathers and the US Constitution, stood up against the king and lords. What guided his thinking? Page 62

9. By faith, Enoch was taken from this life so that he did not experience _____. Page 63

10. Enoch was only one of two who never dies. The other was _____. Page 63

11. Micah 6:8 tell us what the Lord requires of us besides do justly, to love mercy … and what? Page 64

12. At the end of the book of Revelation, Christ is walking among the seven candlesticks. What do they represent? Page 64

13. Enoch knew, "As long as my son is living, God is holding back judgment." Why does God delay? He would rather bring rescue instead of judgment. Page 65

14. God's judgment is described as _____ and _____ to God. Page 66

15. God will judge the world just like He did in Noah's day, but His preference is _____ . Page 66

16. "...You are a gracious and compassionate God, slow to _____ and _____ __ _____ , a God Who relents from sending calamity..." Jonah 4:2 (NIV) Page 67

17. List the 4 attributes of God listed on Pages 67-68.

18. Page 68 says you were made to _____ _____ _____.

19. Have ever felt like you were taking a walk with God? When and how did that feel?

Footnotes for Chapter Five

27. Robert Alter, Genesis: Translation and Commentary (New York: W. W. Norton & Company, 1996). 487
28. Norman Geisler. Systematic Theology, (Ada, MI, Bethany House, 2011) Vol 2., 536.

CHAPTER 6
GOD'S BROKEN HEART

In the book of Genesis, we've learned some of the most foundational principles of our faith:

1. The corrupting nature of sin
2. Sin causes us to be alienated from God, ourselves, and one another.
3. If you leave sin unchecked, it will lead to increasingly violent reactions.

In this chapter, we will learn about God intervening in a world spiraling out of control. This is one of the most famous and also controversial passages in all the Bible. This is a dreadful story and whoever the first person was to sentimentalize this story needs to have their head examined. For those who have trouble believing this story, I want to say that this story or a version of it has been told all over the world.

"It has long been known that legends of a great flood, in which almost all men perished, are widely diffused over the world..." James George Frazer, Folk-Lore in the Old Testament (29)

Even though there are some differences, it's remarkable what these flood stories hold in common. I have heard many skeptics over the years use the fact of multiple stories as evidence to claim it's just a myth. I believe it actually gives evidence that it happened as shown by the percentage of what has been common in these narratives.

Percentage of Information Contained in Flood Stories

Is there a favored family? 88%
Were they forewarned? 66%
Is flood due to the wickedness of man? 66%
Is catastrophe only a flood? 95%
Was flood global? 95%
Is survival due to a boat? 70%
Were animals also saved? 67%
Did animals play any part? 73%
Did survivors land on a mountain? 57%
Was the geography local? 82%
Were birds sent out? 35%
Was the rainbow mentioned? 7%
Did survivors offer a sacrifice? 13%
Were specifically eight persons saved? 9% (30)

If you were to take a composite of what these stories share in common, this is how it might read:

"Once there was a worldwide flood, sent by God to judge the wickedness of man. But there was one righteous family which was forewarned of the coming flood. They built a boat on which they survived the flood along with the animals. As the flood ended, their boat landed on a high mountain from which they descended and repopulated the whole earth."

Why are their flood stories scattered all over the world? Even if the story is told in a culture as a myth, anthropologists tell us that a myth is often a faded memory of a real event.

Details can be lost, added, or even obscured in the constant retelling of the story. Most of history was not shared as written but spoken. Anthropologists also believe that if just two cultures share a similar story from their history, then their ancestors must have a shared experience of that event. One can easily conclude apart from Scripture that the human race seems to have descended from a handful of people who survived a world-wide flood.

The Condition of the World

"When human beings began to increase in number on the earth and daughters were born to them, the sons of God saw that the daughters of humans were beautiful, and they married any of them they chose. Then the Lord said, 'My Spirit will not contend with humans forever, for they are mortal; their days will be a hundred and twenty years.'" Genesis 6:1-3 (NIV)

This activity of sons of God being with daughters of men seemed to be a problem with God. But who are they, these Sons of God and daughters of men?

The Bible doesn't define the Sons of God and the daughters of men, but here are three dominant views:

•The line of Seth and the line of Cain

This theory purports it was a mixing of Seth's godly line with the ungodly line which had poisoned the godly line. Instead of unbelievers becoming believers because of these unions, believers became corrupted.

•The kings of the earth and the daughters of men

These would be ungodly kings who would take any woman they wanted. This took polygamy to a whole new level.

•The fallen angels and daughters of men

This theory was held by early Church Fathers like Tertullian, Justin Martyr, Cyprian, and Ambrose. But Jesus said in the New Testament that angels don't marry (Matthew 22:30).

These fallen angels, however, could've possessed men who would have married these women. If this is true, that would be a dark image of the world before the flood. There are a couple of New Testament passages in Second Peter and Jude that seem to indicate that angels were involved here (2 Peter 2:4-6 and Jude 6).

My opinion leans toward this third option. Regardless of which one you believe, all of these three views have this in common: they blur the lines of marriage, which goes against the creation mandate of Genesis 2. Marriage is under attack, and it has been ever since.

Who were the Nephilim?

"The Nephilim were on the earth in those days—and also afterward—when the sons of God went to the daughters of humans and had children by them. They were the heroes of old, men of renown." Genesis 6:4

Nephilim is a transliteration. It takes the Hebrew word and puts it in English letters. The root word is *nephas,* which means to "fall." They were known, not only because of their stature but because they used their power in malicious ways. Think of them as leaders who became tyrants. Not only is marriage under attack, but the leaders have gotten out of control. And God's verdict is that society is idolizing them as "heroes." In Genesis 4, we learned about how evil violence is, and now they are making heroes out of violent men.

The Grief Violence Caused

"The LORD was sorry that He had made man on the earth, and He was grieved in His heart." Genesis 6:6 (NASB)

The word translated "grieved" is used in the Old Testament to express the most intense emotion: sometimes anguish, sometimes rage mixed with anguish. This word was used to describe how Dinah's brothers felt when they discovered their sister was raped. This is the word used to describe how Jonathan felt when he discovered that his father wanted to kill David. This is the word Isaiah used to describe how a woman feels when her husband deserts her. Notice how God has a deeply personal response to sin. God is emotionally involved with us—He feels love and hate, joy and anger, grief and gladness. Do you remember the shortest verse in the Bible? "Jesus wept." These two words tell us so much about God.

There is a deliberate parallel in Genesis 6 with Genesis 1. Do you remember the refrain? **God created and then He saw that it was good.** In Genesis chapter 6 we see the parallel, however it's an opposite refrain. Again and again what He saw was not good. **What He saw was evil and wicked in every way.** This is why God sent the flood. Remember in Genesis 1:2, "and the Spirit of God was hovering over the waters." (NIV) The first image we have of the pre-formed earth is a planet covered in water. Therefore, He's taking this world back to it's pre-formed state. He's taking back that creation that has become the opposite of what He's meant it to be, and He's going to recreate the creation.

God's Judgment Upon Humankind

After a hurricane struck Haiti in 2010, which killed around 200,000 people, a TV evangelist claimed it was God's punishment for a country that made a pact with the Devil. (31) another TV evangelist said that the attack on 9-11 was God's judgment for harboring abortionists, feminists, and the ACLU. (32)

I could go on and on with examples of Christians who make declarations about God's involvement in catastrophes. These statements are about who God is and how God acts. However, we must square this with Scripture. We believe that God judges, but we need to understand how He judges. If God is judging a people it's always clear where it came from and what it's about. Otherwise, I would not know how to respond to it or be delivered from it.

Moses writes about five cases of God's specific divine judgment: The Flood, Sodom and Gomorrah, the Egyptians, the Canaanites, and the Amalakites. This is what we can learn from these judgments:

- Judgments are always for publicly-recognized cruelty and violence of an extreme and widespread nature.
- Secondly, these judgments are preceded by long periods of warning and exposure to the truth. Why? Because God wants to change the outcome.
- Thirdly, innocent adults are given a way out. If these three things aren't present, it is maligning the character of God to attribute some tragedy to God.

God Does Nothing Without First Knowing All the Facts

God already knows everything because He is omniscient. However, we discover in Scripture a way of describing God's activity in human terms. This is called an anthropomorphism. It helps us with our limited human understanding to have an idea about what God is doing. The idea of God investigating is an example in this story:

"The Lord saw how great the wickedness of the human race had become on the earth, and that every inclination of the thoughts of the human heart was only evil all the time." Genesis 6:5 (NIV)

"Now the earth was corrupt in God's sight and was full of violence. God saw how corrupt the earth had become, for all the people on earth had corrupted their ways." Genesis 6:11-12 (NIV)

"So God said to Noah, 'I am going to put an end to all people, for the earth is filled with violence because of them.'" Genesis 6:13 NIV)

He gathered evidence before He rendered a verdict. Remember in the last chapter we saw that this warning started with Enoch and continued to Methuselah, which means, "When he dies, judgment will come." The reason he lived almost 1,000 years is because God is so patient, and slow to anger…

Noah arrived on the scene and 849 of those years have passed. In Noah's time, there are 120 years left. Therefore, no one could say, "God, if I only had another 400 years I might've seen the error of my ways!"

What Happened to Trigger Such a Drastic Judgment?

It comes down to His verdict on violence. Like then, today we've lost our critique on violence. God is going to destroy what is destroying itself already. It's a play on words in the Hebrew language: the words "corrupted" and "destroy" are the same words:

"...all the people on earth had corrupted their ways...I am surely going to destroy both them and the earth." Genesis 6:12-13 NIV)

It could read: "All the people on earth were self-destructing. Civilization was already destroying itself from the inside out and God was merely recognizing that reality."

What was the original creation mandate? Fill the earth with life: The initial creation mandate was not only unfulfilled but completely reversed. Violence is the opposite of life; they are filling the earth with death.

There is Always a Way of Escape

Grace is always available in our darkest hours

"But Noah found favor in the eyes of the Lord." Genesis 6:8

That word "favor" is the Old Testament word for "grace." This is the first occurrence of the word "grace" in the Bible. Despite what's going on in the world, there's no place so dark that His light cannot illuminate it. Grace is ours for the asking.

What is it about Noah that made him unlike others?

"Noah was a righteous man, blameless among the people of

his time and he walked faithfully with God." Genesis 6:9

Noah was the first human being to be called "righteous." We need to understand this—there's always only been one way that a person can be declared righteous. It's not your sinlessness. It's not the moral achievements of your life. It's faith in the Lord that makes us righteous. Paul makes this point about the next person who is declared righteous, which was Abraham.

"In the same way, Abraham believed God, and God counted him as righteous because of his faith. The real children of Abraham, then, are those who put their faith in God." Galatians 3:6-7 (NLT)

In Galatians, they had a bunch of people there saying, "We are children of God because we've been circumcised. We are Jews; we are family!" In Genesis 17, Abraham was circumcised. However, Paul goes back to Genesis 15:6 which says, "Abraham believed the Lord, and he credited to him as righteousness." (NIV) This was also 430 years before the Law was given. In other words, you are not declared righteous because of what you do. You are declared righteous because of who you believe. Noah believes God and is declared righteous.

God is a Promise-Making, Promise-Keeping God.

"But I will establish my covenant with you, and you will enter the ark—you and your sons and your wife and your sons' wives with you." Genesis 6:18 (NIV)

This is another first: the first occurrence of the word "covenant" in the Bible.

A covenant is a binding contract between two people. The good news is that the covenant that God makes is unbreakable and everlasting. We are in a relationship with a committed God. Again, the foundational principle is that He does not change. This covenant was not Noah's idea—it was God's idea. He announces judgment, but with Noah, He establishes His covenant. He didn't say, "Noah, if you do your part, I will establish My covenant." This is less about cooperation and more about the faithfulness of God. God will never forsake Noah, even if Noah is faithless.

God swears oaths by Himself throughout Scripture. "I am making this promise based on MY character that I will keep it." This is the opposite of the way we tend to think of covenants. We think of it as a two-way promise, but He doesn't make us swear an oath to Him.

We are introduced to the ark at the end of this chapter. The word "ark" only appears in one other place in the Bible, which is in the Exodus story. When they threatened to slaughter all of the Hebrews, and baby Moses escaped slaughter by being floated down the Nile in a little waterproof box, the same word is used. The Hebrew word for "ark" is not boat, but box. God instructs Noah to cover the ark with pitch, which is like tar, and makes it waterproof. And the word used for covering the ark is the same word that means to atone or to cover with the price of redemption.

Noah was asked to build an ark where there is a complete covering for everyone inside.

The dimensions: 450 ft. long, 75 ft. wide, and 45 ft. high. Its length is ten times its height. It's about the size of a small battleship or a cargo boat. It was 95,700 square feet and could hold 35,000 different varieties of species and seven people plus food for a year.

It may surprise you that something of this size only had one door. And once you have the foundational principles from Genesis, you realize this is one of the most explicit references to the Gospel in Genesis.

The Plan

- Early on, we had the first promise of the Messiah in Genesis 3.
- The seed of woman would rise up and crush the serpent's head.
- And now in this chapter: human beings have sinned. They deserve God's judgment.
- Still, God is patient and merciful. He makes the path of escape clear to anyone who repents and believes. His heart breaks for us because He has a great love for us.
- It's faith in God that renders us righteous.
- God offers a covenant for those who believe and swears by Himself that He will keep it.
- If you want to escape the judgment, there's a door that is open to you; and once you enter, you will find yourself covered, protected, and assured that God has done everything to save you from the judgment you deserve.
- The Uncreated has created a path to redemption, and you become a brand new creation.

"Therefore, if anyone is in Christ, the new creation has come:[a] The old has gone, the new is here!" 2 Corinthians 5:17 (NIV)

And God has left for Himself this witness in every culture…

Growing Roots Deeper

Chapter 6 Questions for Bible Study

1. Sin causes us to be alienated from ____, _____, and ____ _____.

2. If you leave sin unchecked, it will lead to _____ _____ reactions. Page 73

3. In this chapter, we will learn about God _____ in a world _____ ____ __ _____. This is one of the most famous and also _____ passages in all the Bible. Page 73

4. The great flood story or a version of it has been told all over the world. What one fact appears in 88% of these legends? Page 74

5. Anthropologists tell us that a myth is often a _____ _____ ___ __ _____ _____. Page 74

6. Anthropologists believe that if just two cultures share a similar story from their history, then their ancestors must have a _____ _____ of that even. Page 75

7. This activity of sons of God being with daughters of

men seemed to be a problem with God. But who are they, these Sons of God and daughters of men? Which theory do you think is viable? Pages 75 – 76

8. "The LORD was sorry that He had made man on the earth, and He was grieved in His heart." Genesis 6:6 (NASB) What does the word (translated) "grieved" mean? Page 76

9. God is emotionally involved with us—He feels love and hate, joy and anger, grief and gladness. What does the shortest verse in the Bible say? Page 77

10. What is the deliberate parallel in Genesis 6 with Genesis 1? Page 77

11. Moses writes about five cases of God's specific divine judgment: The Flood, Sodom and Gomorrah, the Egyptians, the Canaanites, and the Amalakites. What can we learn from these judgments? Page 78

12. "But Noah found _____ in the eyes of the Lord."
Genesis 6:8 Page 80

13. That word "favor" is the Old Testament word for
"_____." This is the first occurrence of the word
"_____" in the Bible. Page 80

14. Despite what's going on in the world, there's no
place so dark that His light cannot illuminate it.
_____ is ours for the asking. Page 80

15. What is it about Noah that made him unlike others?
Page 80-81

16. The real children of Abraham, then, are those who
_____ _____ _____ ___ _____ put their faith in
God." Galatians 3:6-7 (NLT) Page 81

17. A covenant is a binding contract between two
people. The good news is that the covenant that
God makes is _____ and
_____. Page 82

18. Noah was asked to build an ____ where there is a
complete covering for everyone inside. Page 82-83

19. In the Plan on page 83, circle the part that amazes you the most about God's plan?
    - The time it started
    - The fact God judges
    - What makes man righteous
    - The path to redemption
    - That you can become a new creation

Footnotes for Chapter Six

29. James George Frazer, Folk-Lore in the Old Testament, Vol. 1 (London, England, MacMillan and Company, 1919) 105.
30. Ibid., 106
31. Dan Fletcher, Time Magazine, Thursday, Jan. 14, 2010
32. Web address - www.dailymail.co.uk/home/sitemaparchive/day_2001091 4.html

CHAPTER 7
CREATION 2.0

In the last chapter, we read about how flood stories are known all over the world. Dan Show, a Wycliffe Bible Translator in Papua New Guinea, talks about how even there, they have passed down a flood story through the generations. (33)

Scholar James Montgomery Boice also reports: "In India, the Hindus regard Manu as the progenitor of the race. He had been warned of the pending flood by a fish, who told him to build a ship and load all kinds of seeds, together with seven Rishis, or holy beings. The flood came, and people drowned. But Manu's ship was drawn to safety by the fish which finally caused it to run aground on the highest summits of the Himalayan Mountains. In this story, eight people were saved, and Manu is called 'righteous among his generation.' Even more remarkable, the Hindus preserve a story in which Manu later became drunk and lay uncovered until cared for by two of his sons, a close retelling of the story found in Genesis 9:20–27." - James Montgomery Boice, Genesis (34)

These are just a few more examples of a close re-telling of the Flood account where there is no knowledge of the Scriptural account. When the ancient city of Nineveh was excavated in 1845, they discovered 20,000 clay tablets, and several contained these words:

"The mountain of Nisir stopped the ship. I sent forth a dove, and it left. The dove went and turned, and a resting place it did not find, and it returned." - Clay tablets from the ancient city of Nineveh (35)

This flood story has left its mark on more than 500 different cultures. While the Bible is not just a history book, it shares accurate historical events. We also have to acknowledge that the Bible is not a science book, even though we have seen in chapter 1 how it is closer to science than many people believe. At the same time, we can't get so caught up in trying to tie history and science together with the Bible that we miss its main message. That main message is God's love for us and the lengths which He will go to gather His lost sheep. Science focuses on the "know-how." Scripture focuses on the "know-why."

Augustine, who lived in the 300s A.D., said, "We must be on guard against giving interpretations of Scripture that are far-fetched or opposed to science, and so exposing the Word of God to ridicule of unbelievers."- St. Augustine (36)

"The Spirit of God who spoke through them [authors of the Bible] did not choose to teach about the heavens to men, as it was of no use for salvation."- St. Augustine (37)

In other words, we are told how to go to heaven, not how the heavens go. Science gives theology perspective and theology gives science meaning.

These two disciplines aren't at war, but we don't need to force certain explanations. Here's an example: "The world is firmly established, it cannot be moved..." Psalm 96:10

For years, this verse was used to say that the earth was a

fixed object in space. And when Galileo said, "No, the earth revolves," the church leaders went ballistic. He showed that an interpretation of Scripture was wrong—he didn't prove the Bible wrong, just the interpretation.

In this chapter, a similar struggle of an interpretation seems to be at odds with modern science. However, I first want us to notice that this debate isn't even the point of Genesis 7.

Genesis 7 - Primarily Theological Not Geological

The discipline of Biblical theology connects different themes or doctrines throughout Scripture. That's what we've seen in Genesis—how the writer connects this story to the story of Christ. It also shows us as believers how it becomes our story. In Genesis 7, God beautifully weaves this story as a complement to the creation story.

Echoes of Genesis 1 and 2

Remember, Genesis 1 is a very poetic way of describing creation. There is repetition along with many parallels. Now in this chapter, we can see there are parallels with the Flood.

- Both talk about pain—woman's pain, then God's pain.
- God formed man, then man formed evil.
- Both show human beings walking with God.
- Both Adam and Noah had three boys.
- God said creation is good, then said it is not good.
- Both have animals coming to man.
- Both list animals in the order in which they were created.
- Both stories emphasize the significance of the number seven.
- Both include sacrifices.
- Both include a garden and include the man eating

from the fruit of the vine or tree.
- Both include the man being naked and falling into sin.

30 Parallels - Too Many to Be Accidental

In chapter 8, after the flood, God sent a wind over the earth to dry up the water. In Genesis 1, the Spirit of God hovered over the water. The word "spirit" and the word "wind" are the same word. Noah released a dove to search for dry land. What is the dove a symbol for in the New Testament? The Holy Spirit. The dove was going out over the waters just like in the creation story where the Holy Spirit was hovering over the waters.

Not only are there amazing parallels, but there is also repetition in the Flood story just like in Genesis 1. God is re-creating. The flood takes the earth back to its primordial state we saw in Genesis 1. After the flood, there is a starting over. When Noah got off the ark, what did he do? He built an altar and made a sacrifice to God. Don't miss the message trying to figure out how water could be 20 feet above Mt. Everest.

Why Does this Matter?

Not only is this an echo of creation, but an echo of the message of God that continues throughout the Bible. Remember when Moses led God's people out of bondage in Egypt? What was their first obstacle? The Red Sea. We see this image of God hovering over His people in the form of a cloud. And He had to preserve His people through the flooding waters of the Red Sea just like He preserved His family during the Flood in the ark. The Egyptian soldiers, the wicked ones, the violent ones, what happens to them? They drown.

What was the sin of Noah's day? It's violence. **That's what we've discovered in this book, that God's creation has become the opposite of its purpose. Therefore, God destroys those who are already destroying themselves in the flood.** There are the same elements in the Exodus as in the creation and in the Flood. There is a new creation in Israel like there is with Noah. There are too many parallels to be accidental.

Then shortly after Noah gets off the ark and makes a sacrifice, he sins big time. He gets plastered (That wasn't on the flannel board in Sunday School class.). A similar event happens shortly after creation. Adam and Eve sin big time. God gives birth to a new nation, a new son, Israel. They've been set free from bondage, and what happens in the Wilderness? They sin.

Here's the ultimate parallel:
- God sent His only begotten Son, born of a Virgin.
- The first thing we read about Jesus as an adult is His baptism, into the waters. He passes through the waters. Just like Israel passes through the waters.

"As soon as Jesus was baptized, he went up out of the water. At that moment heaven was opened, and he saw the Spirit of God descending like a dove and alighting on him. And a voice from heaven said, 'This is my Son, whom I love; with him I am well pleased.'" Matthew 3:16-17 (NIV)

Water, God's Spirit, hovering, a dove... Can you hear the echoes?

But here's the difference:
- **Jesus' testing would show that He's not like**

Adam.
He's not like Noah. He's not like Israel.
- **His triumph over the Devil in the wilderness would prove that He is the real second Adam.**
- **He is the One Son of God who will obey God the Father in all ways, including obedience to death on a cross.**

It matters because this is the story God has been telling for all time. And this is our story. When we go through the waters of baptism, the old me dies. And I'm raised to walk in a new life. The Holy Spirit descends on me to live in me to do for me what I could never do on my own. God re-creates me too. Aren't you glad God is in the re-creation business?

"If anyone is in Christ, he is a new creation. The old has passed away; behold, the new has come." 2 Corinthians 5:17 (NIV)

God's Final Warnings

Remember before the flood, His warnings were for almost 1000 years. Enoch told of the coming judgment and even named his son Methuselah, which means, "when he dies, judgment will come." Methuselah became a living, breathing sermon illustration. Then when God told Noah to build the ark, He told them there were 120 years left. Then He makes one final plea.

"Seven days from now I will send rain on the earth for forty days and forty nights." Genesis 7:4 (NIV)

It is impossible to read this and say God judges without warning. God is the ultimate "Slow to Anger Being."

94

The Nature of the Judgment

There's nothing necessarily miraculous about a flood, but this one happened on cue. It was predicted beforehand. It was a supernatural event. It was like the plagues God brought upon Egypt. But in cases like these, the people know how to escape judgment because God had told them and warned them.

Globally Universal or Anthropologically Universal?

I believe that Genesis 6-9 is true. Some believe this flood was world-wide or global. Others believe it affected all human beings but wasn't necessarily global.

This is an "in house" argument. There are many topics concerning Scripture that are debated among well-meaning, thoughtful Christians. Although some Christians can be so passionate about certain topics, they seem to make it a "hill to die on." I do not believe this to be that kind of hill.

B.B. Warfield was asked, "What is Christianity?" I love his answer: "Unembarrassed supernaturalism." - B.B. Warfield, Princeton theologian (38)

He was right. Our confidence in this story being true isn't based on how many other cultures share this story, but rather its based on the same confidence we have in the resurrection of Jesus Christ. God is in charge of the miraculous. God can interrupt history. He can suspend the natural order of things.

The Argument for a Globally Universal Flood

This flood was at least to the height of Mt. Ararat which is

17,000 feet. Between creation and the flood, a canopy covered the earth. There were also waters held in the subterranean deep. The flood, most likely, came from these two sources and the massive flood changed the crust of the earth. At this time many mountain ranges were created, the continents drifted apart and canyons were cut. This all happened 8,000-10,000 years ago.

These are the main arguments for a globally universal flood:

1. The language of Genesis 6-8 is universal:
    *   EARTH (*eretz* or *adâmâh*) is used 42 times
    *   ALL (*kowl*) is used 20 times
    *   EVERY (also *kowl* in Hebrew) is used 23 times
    *   UNDER HEAVEN (literally, "under the sky") is used 2 times

2. The Flood lasted an extraordinary length of time.

3. The construction of an Ark is absurd if it were just a local flood.

4. God promised never again to destroy the earth with a Flood.

The Problems with a Globally Universal Flood

"You set a boundary they [the waters] cannot cross; never again will they cover the earth." Psalm 104:9 (NIV)

When the oceans were formed in creation, God says they would never completely cover the earth. The other struggle is about the mountains rising up from the flood waters. The Bible doesn't really address this. The Bible does talk about mountains before the flood. (Genesis 7:9 and 8:4). The Bible doesn't mention the continents drifting apart either. Some people also argue that God caused angels to deliver some of the animals, that He caused some of them to hibernate during the flood. The difficulty is not that God couldn't do these things, but more that the Bible is silent on these things.

Geologists say that a global flood would require four and a half times the amount of water available on the earth. Other issues: how could fresh water lakes have survived and fresh water fish? How come kangaroos are only in Australia? How could coral survive? How could all animals migrate when some do not because of special diets? What did the carnivores eat? Some say they ate all the unicorns!

The Argument for an Anthropologically Universal Flood

"That the flood was universal as far as man is concerned is made totally final in the Scripture." - Francis Schaeffer (39)

He's right, that is clear in Scripture. We are unclear, however, how vast the Flood actually was. Sometimes we also have to be aware of hyperbolic language in Scripture.

Lake Erie is the smallest of the Great Lakes, and yet it's one hundred times bigger than the Sea of Galilee. It is about thirty miles around. Jerusalem is described as being on a mountain. And having been there, it feels more like a hill to me.

In the Flood account, the word earth can also be translated as land in Hebrew. Great words can be used to describe things that are not exactly as big as the word used. We do this all of the time when we describe things we have witnessed to relay how grand the experience was.

There is evidence of a catastrophic flood in the Middle-East from about 8,000 years before Christ. It turned a fresh water sea, the Baltic Sea, into a salt water sea.

"That such an event actually happened is now absolutely certain, accredited by scientists of international repute to the same degree of confidence with which, only a few years ago, the Noah story was being dismissed as nonsense." - Ian Wilson, *Before the Flood: The Biblical Flood as a Real Event and How It Changed the Course of Civilization.* (40)

"So there can be absolutely no doubt that what Pitman and Ryan had discovered was a veritable Flood of epic proportions." - Ian Wilson, *Before the Flood: The Biblical Flood as a Real Event and How It Changed the Course of Civilization.* (41)

The Problems with an Anthropologically Universal Flood

1. God does make a promise not to destroy the world again.
2. The ark doesn't make sense if they could've just migrated to a safer place.

What Really Matters

No matter you believe about the flood, know that it's not the main point. We must understand what God is doing in this story and how it applies to our life.

"Christians who love the Scripture have discussed at length whether the flood was universal or not. I believe it was, but I do not think by any means that we should make it a 'test of orthodoxy.'" - Francis Schaeffer (42)

The main points in this story are:

- God is always working to redeem.
- It's not based on your will power or on your won't power.
- It's based on God's power to change us with the Gospel.

Do you have a past that needs to be washed away? Come to the fountain of grace.

Growing Roots Deeper

Chapter 7 Questions for Bible Study

1. When the ancient city of Nineveh was excavated in 1845, they discovered 20,000 clay tablets. Several contained words. What did the words say? Page 89-90

2. This flood story has left its mark on more than _____ different cultures. While the Bible is not just a history book, it shares _____ _____ _____. Page 90

3. How many parallels are in chapter 1 and chapter 7? Page 92

4. What was the sin of Noah's day? Page 93

5. We've discovered in this book, that God's creation has become the opposite of its purpose. Therefore, God destroys those who are _____ _____ _____. Page 93

6. After the flood, there is a starting over. When Noah got off the ark, what two things did he do? Page 93

7. What does page 93 call the ultimate parallel?
- God sent His _____ _____ ___ , ____ __ __
  _____ .

- The first thing we read about Jesus as an adult is His baptism, into the waters. He passes through the
  _____ .

8. The Nature of judgment is: the people _____ _____
   __ _____ judgment because God had told them and warned them. Page 95

9. At the time of the flood, many mountain ranges were created, the continents drifted apart and canyons were cut. According to page 96, how long ago did this happen?

10. What are some of the discrepancies with the different theories of the flood? Page 96-98

11. No matter you believe about the flood, know that it's not the main point. We must understand what God is _____ in this story and how it _____ to our life. What really matters? Pages 98

12. There are three main points in this story:
- God is always _____ __ _____.
- It's not based on your ___ _____ __ __ ____

  _____ _____.
- It's based on God's power __ _____ __ ____ ___

  _____. Page 99

13. We all have a past that needs to be washed away. When was a time you felt God's mercy? Come to the fountain of grace and thank Him.

Footnotes for Chapter 7

40. Ian Wilson, Before the Flood: The Biblical Flood as a Real Event and How It Changed the Course of Civilization. New York: St. Martin's, 2002) 8.
41. Ibid, 8.
42. http://www.evidenceunseen.com/articles/science-and-scripture/the-genesis-flood-global-or-local.
43. Global Flood Resources:
    • John Clement Whitcomb, and Henry M. Morris. The Genesis Flood: The Biblical Record and Its Scientific Implications. (Grand Rapids, MI: Baker Book House, 1974).
    • Charles Martin, Flood Legends: Global Clues of a Common Event. (Green Forest, AR: Master, 2009).
    • Norman L. Geisler, Baker Encyclopedia of Christian Apologetics. (Grand Rapids, MI: Baker, 1999). See "Flood, Noah." Archer, Gleason L. A Survey of Old Testament Introduction. Third Edition. (Chicago, IL: Moody, 1998) 214-223.
    • Local Flood Resources:
    • The Noachian Flood: Universal or Local? by Carol A. Hill
    • http://www.csun.edu/~vcgeo005/Carol%201.pdf
    • William Ryan, and W. C. Pitman III. Noah's Flood: The New Scientific Discoveries about the Event that Changed History. (New York, Simon and Schuster. 1998).
    • Ian Wilson, Before the Flood: The Biblical Flood as a Real Event and How It Changed the Course of Civilization. (New York: St. Martin's, 2002).
    • See also http://www.evidenceunseen.com/articles/science-and-scripture/the-genesis-flood-global-or-local/
    • Hugh Ross, The Genesis Question: Scientific Advances and the Accuracy of Genesis. (Colorado Springs, CO, NavPress, 1998).
    • John Walton, Genesis: The NIV Application Commentary. (Grand Rapids, MI: Zondervan, 2001). "The Genesis Flood: Why the Bible Says It Must Be Local."

CHAPTER 8
GOD REMEMBERS

If you were writing someone a letter, an email, or a text and you wanted a part of it to really stand out, how would you do that? Some preachers say, "If you don't get anything else, get this..." Or we repeat it a lot. Some people put that part in all caps. Some use exclamation points. Others use several!!! But modern language demands we use emojis.

But how would someone like Moses make sure the ancient-times-reader knew the main emphasis? He had to write on papyrus. It was mashed up reeds and not readily available. In order to save space and maximize the material, they didn't use punctuation and tried to put as much as possible on each page. How would you emphasize something with limited space and materials to work with?

The Main Emphasis in the Flood Narrative

In Genesis 6-9, there is a chiasmus which was a common way to write back then, especially with the Jewish people. A chiasmus is an inverted parallelism—an ABCCBA arrangement. It builds toward the middle. Therefore, the middle is the most important part.

The Importance of Chiastic Structure

The Song of Songs, also known as the Song of Solomon, is one long chiasmus—the entire book. This Old Testament book is composed of 111 lines that lead up to the center, and then 111 lines that decrescendos after. The first 111 lines are about young love. This couple wants to get married. Crescendo to the center and the honeymoon happens. In the last part, the celebration of married love takes place. The following is the exact middle. The narrative speaks from the perspective of the woman, the man, and friends:

"Awake, north wind, and come, south wind! Blow on my garden, that its fragrance may spread everywhere. Let my beloved come into his garden and taste its choice fruits. I have come into my garden, my sister, my bride; I have gathered my myrrh with my spice. I have eaten my honeycomb and my honey; I have drunk my wine and my milk. Eat, friends, and drink; drink your fill of love." Song of Songs 4:16-5:1 (NIV)

What is the main point of the Song of Songs? It's how to get to the wedding night with your moral purity intact.

Another example of a chiasmus in Scripture is when Jesus preached at the synagogue in Nazareth:

Luke 4:16-22
_(A) went to the synagogue
__(B) stood up to read
___(C) given to Him the book of Isaiah
____(D) He opened the book
_____(E) the Spirit of the Lord is upon Me
_____(F) proclaim Good News to the poor
_____(G) release the captives
_____**(H) recovering of sight to the blind**
_____(G) liberty for the oppressed
_____(F) to proclaim
_____(E) the acceptable year of the Lord
____(D) He closed the book
___(C) gave it back to the attendant
__(B) sat down

_(A) the eyes of all in the synagogue were fixed on Him

This is called the Jubilee declaration. Why is "recovering of sight to the blind" the most important? Do you realize that giving sight to the blind is a miracle that never happened in the Old Testament? However, God's Word talks about it in the Old Testament. God has this power to give sight to the blind.

"The Lord gives sight to the blind, the Lord lifts up those who are bowed down, the Lord loves the righteous." Psalm 146:8 (NIV)

In several places in the Old Testament, it says that God and only God has the power to give sight to the blind. The people began to realize that since God has the power to give sight to the blind, but it wasn't happening, this must be something Messiah will do.

One of the signs of the Messiah is that He will give sight to the blind. Isaiah 61 is one of the great messianic chapters in the Old Testament.

Jesus is preaching in His hometown, when those watching say, "This is the carpenter's kid!" They had been taught this passage that the Messiah would give sight to the blind. But they are blind. They cannot see that Jesus is the Messiah. This is precisely why the message is in the middle. It is so important!

We can through the microscope of history and science aided by the Holy Spirit understand how precise all of Scripture is. It would be impossible for over 40 authors over 1,500 years to share such a consistent message without error.

We also see this chiasmus structure in these four chapters, Genesis 6-9:

Genesis 6-9
_(A) Noah and his world before the flood

__(B) God's covenant
___(C) embarking
____(D) rising waters
_____**(E) "But God remembered Noah"**
____(D) falling waters
___(C) disembarking
__(B) God's covenant
_(A) Noah and his world after the flood

The Central Point

"God remembered Noah." Genesis 8:1 (NIV)

We typically emphasize the flood, but not Moses, the writer of this story. What is in the middle? It's about God's commitment to His people. Even in the midst of tragedy, God doesn't forget us!

"The Hebrew word (remember), especially when used in reference to God, signifies acting on a previous commitment to a covenant partner." – Dr. Bruce Waltke, Genesis: A Commentary (44)

Unlike God, I have a tendency to forget. God knows you and remembers you. Doesn't it feel great to be remembered?

"God is not hurried along in the time-stream of this universe any more than an author is hurried along in the imaginary time of his own novel. He has infinite attention to spare for each one of us. He does not have to deal with us in the mass. You are as much alone with him as if you were the only being he had ever created. When Christ died, he died for you individually just as much as if you had been the only man in the world." That is how personal God's love is. - C.S. Lewis, Mere Christianity (45)

When he was in office, President Herbert Walker Bush was visiting in a nursing home and approached a man walking in the hall. The president took the man's hand and said, "Sir, do you know who I am?" The man stared at him for a minute and finally shook his head and said, "No sir, I don't know who you are—but if you ask the nurses at the desk, I'm sure they can tell you." Even famous people can be forgotten by humanity.

The sections of the Bible that tend to bother most people talk about judgment. Being human, we want to accuse God of being arbitrary and unfair, but what we've seen in the chapters of Genesis, showcases the grace of God that is available in every act of judgment, regardless of the kind of rebellion. We've seen the kindness of God and the slowness of His anger. Genesis shows how He warns the people, giving them an opportunity to turn to Him. We've seen how God gives mercy even when we lie to Him. Therefore, when people charge God with being unfair, they're probably reading Scripture through the lens of hurt.

In this chapter, we read that violence has crept into almost every part of the human race, but not Noah and his family. The Scriptures describe them as righteous, and as we discovered earlier, the only way you can be declared righteous by God is by faith. Declared righteous by God, Noah and his family are the ones who God remembers. This is the first occurrence of the "righteous remnant." And we learn that throughout history, there will always be a remnant who trusts God. And God always preserves the remnant.

There is Always a Way of Escape

In the story of Jericho, we see another example of this way to escape, more specifically in the story of Rahab. Who better represents the corruption of the Canaanites than an Amorite prostitute like Rahab? She represents the seedier side of Canaan, but she also represents the truth when God says, "If you seek me with all your heart, you will find Me."

God tells the Israelites to send in spies. What's the purpose of the spies? They're told to assess the troops and the fortifications. But think about how God was going to defeat this city. Once a day, every day, for six days, walk around the city. On the seventh day, walk around it seven times, blow the trumpet and the walls will fall. Why would you need intelligence on the enemy's fortifications when God is going to destroy the city in that way? What information are they gathering? Perhaps they will discover the Canaanite people hate songs in the key of G? I don't think so, nor does He need spies to assess the enemy's strength.

I believe with all my heart that God sent those spies in for one reason and one reason only. Inside the walls of that doomed city, a sinful woman, a prostitute, who had heard rumors of a God who parted the Red Sea, won battles for His people, and held back the waters of the Jordan river, wanted to know this God. And this God will go to the extreme to save those who seek Him. He always cares about the righteous remnant. Not only does God deliver her, but He grafts her into the very lineage of Jesus Christ, the Messiah. Again, this story of Jericho reflects the same emphasis stressed in the story of the flood—God remembers His kids.

A New Beginning for Humankind

This is a re-creation event. The first thing that happens is:

"...He sent a wind over the earth, and the waters receded." Genesis 8:1b (NIV)

The Lord Sends His Wind

Remember, God did the same thing to part the Red Sea. We also find a progression in these re-creation events. In Genesis 1, He creates a man and a woman. In Genesis 6-9, He re-creates a family. Then when He delivers Israel, they pass through the waters of the Red Sea, and He starts again with a nation. However, it's not set right until Jesus comes as the new Adam and God tells His people to go to the "uttermost parts of the world." (Acts 1:8) Remember Pentecost? One hundred twenty were gathered, and they received the Holy Spirit.

"They were all together in one place. Suddenly a sound like the blowing of a violent wind came from heaven." Acts 2:1-2 (NIV)

We see this repetition. The word "spirit" and the word "wind" in both Greek (*pneuma*) and Hebrew (*ruakh*) are the same word. This connection is undeniable!

Noah was Extremely Patient

"...and on the seventeenth day of the seventh month the ark came to rest on the mountains of Ararat." Genesis 8:4 (NIV)

"By the twenty-seventh day of the second month the earth was completely dry." Genesis 8:14 (NIV)

That is more than six months—six months to learn great patience. I don't know about you, but I don't know if I could be that patient. When I'm on a long flight, after the plane lands, I have my seat belt, my bag in hand. And I'm standing with my neck crooked, thinking real judgmental thoughts about everyone in front of me—anyone who is not as ready to get off the plane as I am. There! That's my confession.

What did Noah do? Noah sent out a raven and the raven did not return to the ark. The Bible says ravens are unclean creatures because they eat the flesh of decaying animals.

Next, he sent out a dove. The dove returned in the evening. He waited a week and sent out the dove again. This time, it returned with an olive leaf.

It was a common practice to carry birds on a ship to figure out their proximity to land. A raven has a longer flying distance. But a dove can only fly about 50 miles. Therefore, Noah knew they were close to land when the dove returned. But Noah still didn't leave the ark until God said:

"Come out of the ark." Genesis 8:16 (NIV)

The First Act in the New Creation

"Then Noah built an altar to the Lord and, taking some of all the clean animals and clean birds, he sacrificed burnt offerings on it." Genesis 8:20 (NIV)

You may wonder how he could make a sacrifice if there were only two of each kind of animal. God actually instructed him to take seven of each animal that was clean. Sometimes the facts of the actual story are skewed by the stories told in Sunday School.

The sacrifice is our response to God remembering us. Noah remembered God.

God Makes a Promise

"Never again will I curse the ground because of humans, even though every inclination of the human heart is evil from childhood. And never again will I destroy all living creatures, as I have done." Genesis 8:21 (NIV)

It's important to understand that the Flood didn't change human nature. Remember, there are hundreds of flood accounts. In the Babylonian account, it says that the gods ended the flood because they were hungry and needed the sacrifice of men. It was the same in the Mesopotamian account—the gods swarmed the sacrifice because they were starving.

These accounts show us the problem with most religions. Most are a projection of humanity's problems. However, the Bible is clear. We don't sacrifice to God because He's hungry. We don't give because He needs our money. We sacrifice to honor the God who remembers us even though we are sinful creatures.

Now we see an amazing insight into the character of God—

when He judges us, it is to destroy what is already destroying us. He still hurts over our sinful nature and grieves.

"...the Lord was sorry...and it grieved him." Genesis 6:6 (NIV)

"With amazing boldness the text invites (us) to penetrate to the heart of God... What we find is not an angry tyrant, but a troubled parent who grieves over the alienation." – Dr. Walter Bruggeman, Genesis (46)

Parents, can you relate? We love the prodigals in our life. Unlike other deities, God isn't enraged, but heart-broken. Many things in this world can make us feel forgotten, but God remembers.

Growing Roots Deeper

Chapter 8 Questions for Bible Study

1. Without emojis how would someone like Moses make sure the ancient-times-reader knew the main emphasis? What was used in Genesis 6-9? Page 105

2. Where is another place in the Bible is the "middle-is-the-most-important-part" used? Page 106-108

3. The sections of the Bible that tend to bother most people talk about _____. Page 109

4. Genesis shows how God warns the people, giving them an opportunity to turn to Him. We've seen how God gives _____ even when we lie to Him. Therefore, when people charge God with being unfair, they're probably reading Scripture through the ___ __ _____. Page 109

5. In the story of Jericho, we see another example of this way to escape, more specifically in the story of Rahab. She represents the _____. She represents the seedier side of Canaan, but she also represents what? Page 109

6. God tells the Israelites to send in spies. What's the purpose of the spies? Page 109-110

7. What happens to this prostitute, Rahab? Page 110

8. The story of Jericho reflects the same emphasis stressed in the story of the flood—God _____ ____ ____. Page 110

9. "...He sent a wind over the earth, and the waters receded." Genesis 8:1b (NIV) What other places are mentioned on 110-111 where God uses the wind?

10. How did Noah know the flood was receding? Page 111

11. What was the first act in the new creation? Page 112

12. How could Noah make a sacrifice if there were only two of each kind of animal? Page 112

13. What was God's Promise? Page 112

14. Parents, can you relate? We love the prodigals in our life. Unlike other deities, God isn't enraged, but _____-_____. Many things in this world can make us feel forgotten, but God _____. Page 113

15. Has there been a time in your life when you felt forgotten?

Footnotes for Chapter 8

44. Bruce K. Waltke, Cathi J. Fredricks Genesis, (Zondervan, Grand Rapids August 1, 2001) 366.
45. C. S. Lewis, Mere Christianity, (New York, Touchstone Books, 1996 (first published 1943)) 14
46. Walter Brueggemann, Genesis (Atlanta: John Knox Press, 1982), p. 307.

CHAPTER 9
GOD'S COVENANT

Remember the chiasmus—an inverted parallelism—the ABCCBA arrangement, where the middle is the most important part. To understand the meaning we must look at what is in the center.

Genesis 6-9 Chiasmus
_(A) Noah and his world before the flood
__(B) God's covenant
___(C) Embarking
____(D) Rising waters
_____**(E) "But God remembered Noah"**
____(D) Falling waters
___(C) Disembarking
__(B) God's covenant
_(A) Noah and his world after the flood

This is another reminder that our God is the God of second chances. Almost everything in this chapter is God speaking except at the end, where we have the only recorded words of Noah.

God is a Covenant-Making, Covenant-Keeping God

God swears an oath to Noah:

"Behold, I establish my covenant with you and your offspring after you, and with every living creature that is with you, the birds, the livestock, and every beast of the earth with you, as many as came out of the ark; it is for every beast of the earth. I establish my covenant with you:

"Never again will all life be destroyed by the waters of a flood; never again will there be a flood to destroy the earth." Genesis 9:9-11 (NIV)

Covenants were typically made by kings called suzerains and lower kings called vassals. These were legally binding agreements ending a war, making and keeping the peace. Each covenant always contained symbols.

The Noahic Covenant
    9:1 preamble and stipulations
    9:1-3 the blessing from God
    9:5-6 the curse
    9:9–11 the oath
    9:12–17 the sign (47)

What does this tell us about God? It tells us: God is personal.

God is Personal

The Hebrew word "covenant" (*berit*) occurs seven times in verses 8-17. He promised to never destroy mankind with a flood. He also promised to protect the food supply in seed and harvest. He talked about preserving life and punishing those who inappropriately take life.

Think about how unique it is that the God of the universe makes a covenant with us. This idea of a personal God is unique among the various worldviews. You hear that fate governs humanity—or that God is unknowable. But the Bible teaches that God wants a relationship with us. He makes promises when He doesn't have to promise us anything. And who does He make promises to? Fallible people, broken people, people who often defy Him. God meets us as we are and where we are.

God Makes an Unconditional Promise

A Suzerainty Covenant is from a king. The king makes the terms, and the people have no choice but to agree. The covenant here is remarkable because it's unconditional. It's one-sided. It does not depend on man's obedience. God does this knowing the world is full of sin—and despite this re-creation, it will be full of sin again. In other words, it is a covenant of grace—not based on merit.

It is also a *b'rith olam*, which is Hebrew for "an everlasting covenant." Therefore, this is for us as much as it was for Noah.

God Gives a Sign of His Covenantal Promise

With Abraham it was circumcision. With the Church in the New Testament, what is it? The bread and wine of Communion. It reminds us that God keeps His promise to save us. In this covenant, it's the rainbow.

The word God uses to describe His symbol is the word "bow," in Hebrew it's *qesheth*. But this word is typically used to describe the bow that goes with an arrow, which as you know is a weapon of war. There's actually another word that is used in Hebrew for rainbow, but it isn't used here.

"Whenever I bring clouds over the earth and the rainbow appears in the clouds, I will remember my covenant between me and you and all living creatures of every kind. Never again will the waters become a flood to destroy all life." Genesis 9:14-15 (NIV)

God is saying, "I am making this promise, my permanent reminder to you. I'm hanging up my bow, and I'm putting it in the sky. The fact that God is hanging up His weapon says a lot about peace, doesn't it? And if it is a bow, what is the orientation of that weapon? It's not aimed at Earth, is it? It is

119

aimed at Himself. Another amazing signpost pointing to the cross.

This is how true peace came to humanity. The weapon of the cross is aimed at Christ. He takes the arrows of our sin into His flesh. Anytime you're discouraged, look up and be reminded that He took your pain.

The bow which symbolizes war now becomes this rainbow which symbolizes peace. God loves to take these weapons of war and turn them into instruments of peace. Both the prophet Isaiah and the prophet Micah repeat this promise word for word:

"He will judge between the nations and will settle disputes for many peoples. They will beat their swords into plowshares and their spears into pruning hooks. Nation will not take up sword against nation, nor will they train for war anymore." Isaiah 2:4 (see also Micah 4:3) (NIV)

God takes what is destructive and turns it into something productive. And He does that with our hearts. God is always working to redeem.

When God gives John the vision of Revelation, do you remember what he sees in heaven? What was surrounding the throne of God? A rainbow, completely encircling it (Revelation 4:3).

It's saying this throne of judgment has become a throne of grace. But do you know the danger of grace? We need it continuously!

Another One Bites the Dust

The biggest surprise in chapter 9 is that the world remains the same. If you thought that God's grace would produce a better world, then just look around you.

We Expect a Different Result

Think about it. If anyone could really know the high price of sin and the value of doing things God's way, it would be Noah and his family. But human beings don't like to admit that we have problems. We are in this vast conspiracy to consider our disreputable behavior as—normal! We are the masters of justifying bad behavior.

Vladimir Putin has often talked about his great hero: Joseph Stalin. There was a famine in Ukraine and when Stalin's wife confronted him about it, he had the students who told her arrested and she then shot herself. Soon afterward, Stalin starved millions of his own people in the 1930s. It is called the Great Terror. When questioned about this, Putin said, "Well in other countries, worse things have happened!" (48)

Noah walked with God. He's a righteous man according to Scripture, and yet he fails. This is another part of the story we often don't share in Sunday School, but the Bible was not written like a fairy tale. It is about real people who had real struggles.

Noah Stumbles

"Noah, a man of the soil, proceeded to plant a vineyard. When he drank some of its wine, he became drunk and lay uncovered inside his tent." Genesis 9:20-21

Noah was the first known to plant vineyards and create wine, which is called viniculture.

This is the first mention of wine in the Bible. Matthew Henry, when he summarized the irony of this chapter, said, "Noah lived soberly when he was surrounded by drunkenness, but he became drunken when he was surrounded by sobriety." – Matthew Henry (49)

This is not the fault of wine, it's the fault of human beings:

that we far too easily abuse God's gifts. Remember we discovered there are hundreds of flood stories all over the world? Almost all of the other stories outside the Bible say that the main character was so good that God just took him to heaven after the flood. The Biblical account tells us the opposite. He's not a man that's obtained perfection, but he's a broken man.

Just about every time we read about a hero in the Bible that we are supposed to emulate, we then see that they fall. This is one of the reasons I love the Bible so much, and I trust it. It tells the truth about its heroes, even when it makes them look bad. It tells us the truth, and it allows us to enter into the story. At this point, something truly bizarre happens:

"Ham, the father of Canaan, saw his father naked and told his two brothers outside. But Shem and Japheth took a garment and laid it across their shoulders; then they walked in backward and covered their father's naked body. Their faces were turned the other way so that they would not see their father naked." Genesis 9:22-23 (NIV)

What just happened?

There is a curse that comes as a result of this incident. What did Ham do? Was it just that he saw his father naked? There would be many people in big trouble in that case! What about those hospital gowns? Here's another example:

"Woe to him who makes his neighbors drink...in order to gaze at their nakedness." Habbakuk 2:15 (NIV)

"The word used for Ham's 'seeing' is not just a glance or something accidental, but a stare." -Dr. Bruce Waltke, Genesis (50)

This word for seeing intently is an important word. Remember when Eve "sees" that the tree is good for food? She wants what is forbidden. In Genesis 6, the Sons of God, "see" the Daughters of Men and take them as their bride. In Sodom and Gomorrah, the men are blinded because they "see" the angels and want to have relations with them. Potiphar's wife "sees" Joseph, so there is a lust that goes with this kind of seeing. This is definitely a euphemism. We have a clue in Leviticus.

"If a man lies with his father's wife, he has uncovered his father's nakedness." Leviticus 20:11 (NIV)

Therefore, it's most likely that this sin isn't just looking, but actually lusting after Noah's wife, who may or may not have been his mother.

The Judgment Pronounced on Canaan

"When Noah awoke from his wine and found out what his youngest son had done to him, he said, 'Cursed be Canaan! The lowest of slaves will he be to his brothers.'" Genesis 9:24-25

Instead of cursing Ham, Noah curses Ham's son. Why? Some scholars suggest that this son could've been the offspring of this incestuous union. There are echoes of the creation account here as well. There's nakedness and shame and it needed a covering, which happened when the brothers covered Noah.

Here's another first—one human curses another human. And Canaan becomes the father to the Canaanites. And the Canaanites developed their religion based on perversion (See Leviticus 18). And we learn that Canaan's brother is Mizraim which is also translated - Egypt, the father of the Egyptians. In Genesis 9, we are beginning to see how the key characters in the Exodus came about. Chapter 9 doesn't end with a curse, but with a blessing.

"Praise be to the Lord, the God of Shem! May Canaan be the slave of Shem. May God extend Japheth's territory; may

Japheth live in the tents of Shem, and may Canaan be the slave of Japheth." Genesis 9:26-27 (NIV)

Shem, Noah's youngest son becomes the chosen one. Usually, it's the first born that gets all the rights, all the inheritance. This is another example of the reversal of primogeniture. God, again, does the unexpected.

Shem's name means "name" because God is literally making a name for Himself: Shem is the ancestor of Abraham.

The Story is Stuck on Repeat

As we've seen already in Genesis, the parallels are obvious. Adam was the father of the human race; Noah is the new father of the re-created human race:

1. The Lord planted a garden in Eden. Adam tried the forbidden fruit and they were naked and ashamed.
2. Noah was a man of the soil. The word "soil" is *adamah*—"ground" or "earth." Noah's forbidden fruit was the wine he made. Most Rabbis believe the forbidden fruit in the garden was a grape rather than an apple. The garden was planted.
3. The fruit of the garden was taken in a forbidden way; their nakedness needed to be covered.

And it repeats with us. There's only one way to break that loop:

"There is therefore now no condemnation for those of us who are in Christ Jesus." Romans 8:1 (NIV)

The weapon was aimed at God. He took the arrows of my guilt and my shame.

Growing Roots Deeper

Chapter 9 Questions for Bible Study

1. What is the most important part of Genesis 6-9 according to the chiasmus on page 117?

2. God is a _____-Making, _____-Keeping God. Page 117

3. God talked about preserving ____ and punishing those who inappropriately take _____. Page 118

4. What does the Noahic Covenant tell us God is _____? Page 118

5. This idea of a personal God is unique among the various _____. Page 118

6. B'rith olam is Hebrew for "an _____ covenant." Therefore, this is for ____ as much as it was for Noah. Page 119

7. God gives a sign of His covenantal promise. With Abraham it was _____. With the Church in the New Testament, it is _____ and _____ of _____. Page 119

8. It reminds us that God keeps His promise to ____ ___. In this covenant with Noah, God's covenant

symbol is the _____. Page 119

9. The weapon of the _____ is aimed at Christ. He takes the arrows of ___ ____ into His flesh. Anytime you're discouraged, look up and be reminded that He took your ____. Page 119-120

10. God takes what is _____ and turns it into something _____. And He does that with our hearts. God is always working to _____. Page 120

11. When God gives John the vision of Revelation, what does he see in heaven, surrounding the throne of God? (Revelation 4:3). Page 120

12. But human beings don't like to admit that we have problems. We are in this vast conspiracy to consider our disreputable behavior as—normal. We are the masters of justifying ____ _____. Page 121

13. Noah is a righteous man according to Scripture, and yet he ____. His son sins. Page 121

14. As we've seen already in Genesis, the parallels are obvious. _____ was the father of the human race; _____ is the new father of the re-created human race. Page 124

15. How has God recreated our heart? Is there an area in your life where you want God's power?

Footnote for Chapter 9

47. Jeffrey J. Niehaus, "Covenant and Narrative, God and Time," Journal of the Evangelical Theological Society 53, no. 3 (2010): 541–542.
48. http://thinkagainonline.com/stalins-wife-commits-suicide.
49. https://www.biblegateway.com/resources/matthew-henry/ genesis.
50. Bruce K. Waltke, Cathi J. Fredricks Genesis, (Zondervan, Grand Rapids August 1, 2001) 387.

CHAPTER 10
MORE BEGATS

If I could only take one chapter of the Bible with me to a desert island, it probably wouldn't be chapter 10. It reads kind of like a telephone book without the numbers. This is a genealogy, but it also contains tribes, nations, and people groups. We've already covered one genealogy in this study and this is the second. This one is about the development of nations.

Dr. Leupold gives hints on how to preach on each passage in his commentary. "It may very well be questioned whether a man should ever preach on a chapter such as this." - Dr. H. C. Leupold, *Genesis* (51)

Dr. James Montgomery Boice, however, preached from this chapter 3 times. He came to the opposite conclusion: "...this is surely one of the most interesting and important chapters in the entire Word of God." - Dr. James Montgomery Boice, *Genesis* (52)

No Other Passage Like Genesis 10 in All the Ancient World

This is a statement from a biblical scholar, who happens to be an unbeliever: "...it stands absolutely alone in ancient literature, without a remote parallel, even among the Greeks, where we find the closest approach to a distribution of peoples in genealogical framework...The Table of Nations remains an astonishingly accurate document." - William F.

Albright, American archaeologist, biblical scholar (53)
Most archaeologists and apologists love chapters like this in the Bible because it establishes and confirms history. Apologetics comes from a Latin word that means, "to defend," as in defending the faith. A powerful principle we need to know when studying apologetics: It's almost impossible to establish a lie in the midst of a known history. And there is no document in history like Genesis 10.

Its Uniqueness – No Mention of Israel

Since the focus in Genesis is on one nation in particular, Israel, you would think Israel would be the focus—the main topic of the chapter, but Israel is not mentioned at all in this chapter. Why? In just two more chapters, the story of Abraham is told. Chapter 12 shows how God chose the one who is considered the father of the nation.

I believe a theological point is being made. I believe God is underscoring the fact that He is the God of the whole world. He's not just the God of Israel. He is the God of the Gentiles too. This is good news for us!

World History

There are exactly 70 names listed. This doesn't count the ones in brackets in verse 14 because they don't belong to the main list. 70 is an important number: Exodus 24 and Numbers 11 talk about 70 elders in Israel. By the time we get to the New Testament, this group morphs into the Sanhedrin, which was the Jewish high court. Jesus also sent out 70 disciples in His ministry. The number 70 has a sacred meaning in the Bible that is made up of the factors of two perfect numbers—7 (representing perfection) and 10, (representing completion).

I believe this is God's way of saying, "There is a perfect, spiritual ordering to the nations of this world." This chapter is about what happened with Noah's three sons once they left the ark. And their offspring developed into clans and tribes and nations. Some of them were friendly to Israel, and some were not. It's not just history, it's also our family tree. We can all find our roots somewhere in Genesis 10.

For many years, a lie perpetuated by hate explained the "curse on Cain" was about skin color. However, Genesis 10 puts that lie to rest. Race is not a factor.

I have always admired a long-time professor at Southwestern Baptist Theological Seminary, Dr. T.B. Maston. He taught ethics there many years before my time at Southwestern. I loved reading his books and learning that he would stand for the truth even when it was not popular. His book, *The Bible and Race,* was written in 1959 when many churches in the South taught that black people were a result of the curse of Cain or the curse of Canaan. He explained in detail how this is not what Scripture teaches. I have often wondered how much he was persecuted for repudiating these then popular beliefs. (54)

Descendants of Japheth (verses 2-5)

They mainly migrated North and West. They traveled the furthest away from where they were born and many settled in Europe. Some settled in India. Linguists have confirmed that European languages and languages in India share a common root. This chapter in Genesis is the only place that established this connection.

Descendants of Ham (verses 6-20)

Ham's descendants were the ones who lived nearest to Israel and almost all of them became enemies: Sodom and Gomorrah, Canaan, Cush, Babylon, Assyria, Nineveh, Philistines, Hittites, Amorites, the bagel bites and the mosquito bites (Sorry, I couldn't resist!).

Cush settled in what is now Ethiopia. We will study his

notorious son, Nimrod, in this chapter.

Descendants of Shem (verses 21-31)

Shem's descendants are the Hebrew nations. The modern term "Semitic" literally means "descended from Shem." But Shem's lineage is actually broader than just the Jewish people. One descendant is Eber and his name is the root of the word "Hebrew." One of his sons, Peleg, is the great-great-great-grandfather of Abraham, who is the father of Israel.

Having finished the difficulties of the "begats," we can now try to understand the implications of this chapter.

The Spiritual Condition of the Nations

People easily forget the one true God. What was the emphasis of the flood narrative? "God remembered Noah." And yet we forget. There's a phrase in verse 1 in the beginning of this chapter and verse 32 in ending of the chapter: "after the flood."

If you thought sin would go away just because God re-creates after the flood, look around you. Remember, Mayberry never was! We have some clues in the person named Nimrod. But first we have to clear up something:

In the English language, this name, Nimrod, has been completely changed from the original Biblical name. Do you know who messed it up? Bugs Bunny calls Elmer Fudd, Nimrod (facetiously because it actually means mighty hunter). We tend to think it means idiot because Elmer Fudd is an idiot. Even most dictionaries say it means an idiot or a jerk.

Nimrod was called "the mighty one." The last time we saw this term was in Genesis 6, talking about the Nephilim, these giants of men were incredibly evil and society idolized them.

Nimrod is just like the Nephilim.

Nimrod is the father of two nations: Babylon and Nineveh. Nineveh becomes the capital of Assyria. They also became Israel's two biggest enemies.

If you trace the word Babylon in the Bible, you discover that it is more than just an empire. It becomes a symbol of any system that exalts human beings above God and runs over anyone who stands in the way.

Even though this chapter does define Nimrod as a mighty hunter, this doesn't mean he was just a good hunter during deer season. He is a hunter of men. This description means "...a violent invasion of the persons and rights of men." - George Bush, *Notes on Genesis* (55)

"[Nimrod] was a bold man, and of great strength of hand; and he gradually changed the government into tyranny, seeing no other way of turning men from the fear of God, but to bring them to a constant dependence on his own power." - Josephus, 1st Century Jewish Historian (56)

Nimrod's name literally means rebel. He really is an archetype. He is what so many have become in history: Caesars, Hitler, Stalin and more. In the next chapter, we see Nimrod as the driving force behind the Tower of Babel.

People Easily Forget the Oneness of the Human Race

We are all created in God's image, and we all descended from the same family. This is biblical theology: the brotherhood of mankind. Paul said in his sermon at Athens: "From one man he made all the nations, that they should inhabit the whole earth; and he marked out their appointed times in history and the boundaries of their lands." Acts 17:26 (NIV)

This is another principle that helps us to understand why

racial prejudice has no place in biblical Christianity. Of course, there are differences in the races, but as real and as profound as they are, it doesn't change the truth: "Human DNA is so stable that you can take two people from any place on earth, compare their DNA, and it will be 99.8% identical. Furthermore, of the 0.2% difference, the visible characteristics (such as skin color, eye shape, and so on) account for only 0.012% of the genetic difference." (57)

We all share that we are greatly fallen and deeply loved. One of my desires as a pastor is to see more diversity within our churches. It has been said that Sunday is the most segregated day of the week. May we all strive to change that as we share the Gospel with everyone, regardless of skin color, race, or any other differences.

God Will Never Forget His Plans for the Entire Human Race

"The world is my parish."- John Wesley, founder of the Methodist Church (58)

Christ told us to go to all nations. When our vision becomes small, when we start worrying about only being around people that are like us, we open ourselves up to the temptation that we are better than others. That is why I repeatedly warn against seeking out Bible study or Life Groups based only on affinity groups. Think about it—most of us who are married have married our opposite. This sometimes creates conflict, but most of us wouldn't change it because we know we can learn so much from people who have a different perspective. In the same way, some of our best teachers are people who come from a completely different background. I believe the success of missionaries is partially based on the differences in cultures. While the barriers are real, the bridges overcome the barriers.

Genesis 10 – Shadows of the Gospel

Israel was chosen to be a channel to bless all nations: "I will also make you a light of the nations so that My salvation may reach to the end of the earth." Isaiah 49:6 (NIV)

"Because mankind is one in its origin, Israel may not pretend that the calling to be a blessing to all the nations is something strange and incomprehensible. Those nations, after all, are their cousins. Those nations are the cousins of the line of Seth. The line of Noah. And of course of the line of Shem." - Cornelius Van Der Waal (59)

Why do you think it took 400 years for the children of Israel to be set free from bondage in Egypt? Did it take them that long to learn a lesson? No, I believe something greater was going on here. As we saw before the flood, God was giving the Canaanites 400 years to repent.

In Acts 8, Phillip encounters the Ethiopian eunuch who is reading Isaiah 53. Phillip asks him if he understands it, and the eunuch says, "No, how can I if no one explains it to me?" Phillip then preaches Christ to him and he was baptized. Do you see that this was a descendant of Ham? His people were enemies to Israel, but now he's included in the family of God.

When Solomon dedicated the temple, he says this in his prayer: "....when the foreigner, who does not belong to your people Israel but has come from a distant land because of your name—when he comes and prays toward this temple, then hear from heaven, your dwelling place, and do whatever the foreigner asks of you, so that all the peoples of the earth may know your name and fear you, as do your own people Israel..." 1 Kings 8:41-43 (NIV)

God's prophets in the Old Testament didn't just preach to Israel, but to the other nations.

Paul also said: "I am under obligation both to Greeks and to the barbarians... the gospel is the power of God for the salvation of everyone who believes, to the Jew first and also to the Greek..." Romans 1:14-16 (NIV)

He then said at Mars Hill that "God: "...made every nation of men, that they should inhabit the whole earth; and he determined the times set for them and the exact places where they should live." Acts 17:26 (NIV)

He's going back to Genesis 10. But realize he's preaching to confirmed racists. They believed the world was divided into two classes—Greeks and Barbarians. And the people hearing this in Athens think they are the best of the Greeks as well. Even Paul was, at one time, a racist. He called himself a Hebrew of the Hebrews. This was a common superlative declaration. He also once believed in two classes: Jews and Gentile "dogs." But after he trusted in Christ, he read Genesis 10 in a new light.

Remember the reluctant prophet, Jonah? God sends him to Nineveh and he doesn't want to go. Why? He doesn't want them to repent and receive God's forgiveness.

"You can, safely assume you've created God in your own image when it turns out he hates all the same people you do." Anne Lamott (60)

If you're ever going to understand who God is, you must understand that God's disposition towards the whole world is love. As His Church, He wants to expand our hearts, so we also see the world in that way.

Jonah is a microcosm of what Israel failed to be. They failed at being light.

Jonah eventually goes to Nineveh, but he takes a bad attitude, preaches the worst sermon ever, and still—the whole nation repents. The Bible says even the cows were covered in sackcloth and ashes.

You see the deeper we make that line in the sand, the less likely we are to ever cross that line. And we really don't comprehend how much God works to help us become light in this dark world. Genesis 10 is here for a reason, so don't skip it.

Growing Roots Deeper

Chapter 10 Questions for Bible Study

1. Genesis 10 is about the development of _____.
   Page 129

2. An unbeliever, William F. Albright, American archaeologist and biblical scholar said: "...it (Genesis 10) stands absolutely alone in ancient literature, without a remote parallel, even among the Greeks, where we find the closest approach to a distribution of peoples in genealogical framework...____ _____ ___ _____ remains an astonishingly accurate document." Page 129

3. Page 130 underscores the fact that He(God) is the God of the _____ _____. He's not just the God of Israel. He is the God of the _____ too.

4. We can all find our roots somewhere in _____ ___. Page 131

5. The modern term "Semitic" literally means "descended from _____." Page 132

6. Nimrod is the father of two nations: _____ and _____. Nineveh becomes the capital of Assyria. They also became Israel's two biggest _____. Page 133

7. _____ becomes a symbol of any system that

exalts human beings above God and runs over anyone who stands in the way. Page 133

8. Josephus, a first Century Jewish Historian says, "[Nimrod] was a bold man, and of great strength of hand; and he gradually changed the government into _____..." Why did Nimrod do this? Page 133

9. "Human DNA is so stable that you can take two people from any place on earth, compare their DNA, and it will be ___.__% identical..." Page 134

10. We all share that we are greatly _____ and deeply _____. Page 134

11. Christ told us to go to all nations. When our _____ becomes small, when we start worrying about only being around people that are like us, we open ourselves up to the what temptation? Page 134

12. God's prophets in the Old Testament didn't just preach to Israel, but to the _____ _____. Page 135

13. When God forces Jonah to go to Nineveh with a bad attitude and preaches the worst sermon ever, what happens? Pages 136-137

14. Has there been a Nineveh in your life? Why and how did you react to your Nineveh?

Footnote for Chapter 10

51. H. C. Leupold, Exposition of Genesis: Volumes 1 & 2, (Grand Rapids, MI, Baker Books, 2010) 380

52. James Montgomery Boice, Genesis: Volume One, (Grand Rapids, MI, Baker Books, 1982) 418.

53. https://enduringword.com/commentary/genesis-10.

54. T.B. Maston, The Bible and Race, (Nashville, TN, Broadman Press, 1959).

55. George Bush, Notes on Genesis (New York, Ivison & Phinney, 1859) 411.

56. https://bible.org/seriespage/lesson-22-roots-nations-genesis-101-32.

57. Leslie Becker, http://gimmeinfo.com/a-house-divided-cannot-stand.

58. http://www.christianitytoday.com/history/people/denominationalfounders/john-wesley.html.

59. Cornelius Van Der Waal, The Covenantal Gospel (Neerlandia, Alberta: Inheritance Publications, 1990), 204.

CHAPTER 11
TOWER OF POWER

If I were to ask you, "What is the spirit of Babel?" What would you say? Is it about a desire to reach heaven in our own strength? Is it about overcoming the language barriers? What happened to cause God to intervene in this way? Hopefully, we can answer these questions in this final chapter of this study.

"... the whole world had one language and a common speech." Genesis 11:1 (NIV)

Literally, it says the people had one lip. In the previous chapter, we learned that Noah's sons and their offspring were scattering. However, once they arrived in this area between the Tigris and the Euphrates, this group decided they would go no further.

A Tower is Built (Ziggurat)

This tower was built with bricks. Interestingly, the Hebrews didn't build with bricks. They built with stones. There was a legend that said when God created the world, He gave two angels each a sack of all the stones for the earth, and when one of the angels flew over Israel, the sack broke and so half of the world's rocks ended up in Israel.

In the Plain of Shinar, in the lower Mesopotamian, stones were scarce. This led to the invention of bricks and the use of bitumen (petroleum product like asphalt) instead of mortar.

The precursors to the pyramids, Ziggurats were supposed to represent a mountain where the gods were thought to gather. They called it "the gate of heaven" or a "stairway to heaven." One Ziggurat was labeled as the link between heaven and earth. But these man-made mountains remained off-limits to the people. In building this tower, these off-springs of Noah were redefining God.
They no longer relied on the God who revealed Himself to their forefathers.

John H. Walton in his commentary said, "...people began to envision their gods in human terms. People were no longer trying to be like God, but more insidiously, were trying to bring god down to the fallen level of humanity...it degraded the nature of God by portraying him as having needs." John H. Walton, NIV Application Commentary: Genesis 11

They have a **wrong view of themselves** and a **wrong view of God**: *They are big, God is small.*

"He needs a staircase so He can come down to be with us." Do you know the problem with this? God is then patronized and manipulated. Once you reduce God to a being for your benefit, then God becomes a puppet. This is the spirit of Babel. When I distort God's image, it's because I want to be in charge.

That's why Babel, or Babylon (same word), represents a godless society in rebellion against the one true God. The building of this tower was really the anti-creation.

The Anti-Creation

It begins with this phrase, "Come, let us..."

We learned in the last chapter that Nimrod was the founder of this city and the driving force behind this tower. Remember, his name means "mighty hunter," but it also means "rebel."

So, the people say, "Come, let's make bricks..." Genesis 11.3 (NIV)

"Come, let us build ourselves a city, with a tower that reaches to the heavens, so that we may make a name for ourselves..." Genesis 11:4 (NIV)

This phrase is a distorted echo of creation because this phrase was used by God, "Let us make mankind in our image, in our likeness..." Genesis 1:26 (NIV)

This was a new creation event with no divine blueprint. The problem was that the architect of Babel was a people who wanted to make a name for themselves. Names are important in Scripture. God named Adam. God the Father named the Messiah. Mary gave birth to Him, but God named Him. When the God of creation named people, that name had a special reason behind it.

However, these builders were trying to make a name for themselves, which is another way of saying, "I want to be in charge."

What Was the Sin?

Was there something inherently sinful in the building of the Tower of Babel? The root sins were:
- Disobedience - God told them to fill the earth, yet they stopped in Mesopotamia and decided to build their own kingdom.
- Pride - Seeking significance and immortality in themselves.
- Rebellion - These rebels were bound together in their defiance of God—a coordinated rebellion. This stands at the heart of Genesis 11.
- Perversion of Religion - They wanted to create a throne on par with God Himself. They wanted to bring

God down on their level so they could elevate themselves to His level.

The Lord Came Down - The Structure

Genesis 11:1-9

_A The entire earth had one language
__B there
___C each other
____D come let us make bricks
_____E let us build for ourselves
_____F a city and tower
_____**G the Lord came down**
_____F the city and the tower
_____E which mankind had built
____D come let us mix up
___C each other's language
__B from there
_A the language of the entire earth (62)

Once again, the meaning is in the middle. Why did the Lord come down? Using anthropomorphic language, God came down to investigate. Of course, He already knew what was going on, but this passage uses human descriptions to tell us the story. And what we discover, as always, is His mercy.

The Lord Limits Progress in Order to Limit Damage

Is God afraid? Is he worried?

No! But God knew this was the beginning of the root of all wars, empires, oppression, and division. The sense of foreboding that we find in the text is not because God is insecure, but God knows that the more they push to be above God, the more trouble will come.

"Come, let us go down and confuse their language so they will not understand each other..." Genesis 11:7 (NIV)

Think about how the people formed this rebellion and why. It's a powerful lesson.

Organization (one people) and information (one language) are the keys to human power. Therefore, in order to limit the damage, God had to break up the organization and the information.

What is the consequence?

The Consequence – Babel is a play on words

In the original Akkadian language, which was a Semitic language spoken in Mesopotamia, Babel means "gate of God." But the Hebrew language has a word that sounds just like it and means "confusion." Another term for that is *paronomasia* and means: two words with different meanings that sound similar. We make puns out of them. The message is, "You think you've built the gateway to God, but you have built nothing but confusion. You think you're making a name for yourself, but in the end, it's all babel, it's jibberish!"

And we need to get used to this word, Babel, because it's only being introduced here. This word is used some 200 times in the Bible, which tells us there's more to the story.

BABEL IS A RECURRING PROBLEM

Babylon or Babel is second in importance only to Jerusalem. They are contrasted so often:

- Jerusalem is the city of God.
- Babylon is the city of the devil.

According to the book of Revelation, Babylon will reach its final form at the end of history. Genesis 11 is **a mirror of the modern world.**

How we understand the spirit of Babel or Babylon helps us to understand the world today. The world we live in worships the superlative: good, better, best; big, bigger, biggest. The preoccupation with power comes from a deep-seated insecurity. We reason that if we can be the strongest, the smartest, and have the most, we believe that we won't have to depend on anyone, much less God.

Is it a sin to work hard? No! Is it a sin to achieve? No! But it isn't hard to cross the line from capturing the prize to it capturing you.

Pride is a tricky thing: pride is what made the devil, the devil. This search for significance can lead us to compromise our values, too. We end up lying to everyone including ourselves. We use people as long as they are useful for our purposes and discard them when they don't fit our plans.

Remember, Babylon is about control. It's about uniting a culture against God's values. We have seen in our culture this progression.
- Marginalize God's values.
- Criminalize God's values.

Babylon is about the empire, forcing their will upon the people.

Babylon as a Present and Future Reality

Revelation 17-18 deals with the ultimate destruction of Babylon. Chapter 17 presents Babylon as a prostitute. Babylon is unfaithful. Chapter 18 shows Babylon as an economic reality. In Babylon, the global marketplace will reign supreme. It says in the end-times a leader will emerge who is even stronger than Nimrod, the rebel. He will be called the Anti-Christ. He will lead this consummation of Babylon.

The Bible also says that you will not be able to participate in this system apart from having the Mark of the Beast. Where are you supposed to get it? The forehead or the hand is where it will be. You won't be able to buy or sell without this mark, so it's about economics.

Mark of the Beast

What will this mark be? There are 404 verses in the book of Revelation and 500 references to the Old Testament. This is actually a reference to Exodus 13:9 about the Feast of Unleavened Bread.

"This observance will be for you like a sign on your hand and a reminder on your forehead that this law of the Lord is to be on your lips. For the Lord brought you out of Egypt with his mighty hand." Exodus 13:9 (NIV)

To be marked on your forehead is about your thinking and your attitude. If you are marked on your hand, it's about what you do. This sign says that my thinking and my behavior match up with the faithfulness of God. Therefore, the Mark of the Beast is about one's unfaithfulness to God marked by one's attitude and behavior.

John, who wrote the book of Revelation, is pointing out that there will come a time when God's people will not participate in this world system without pledging loyalty to the beast. Can this happen today? I believe it is already happening. With every new thing introduced into our lives, ask the question, "What will human depravity do with this?"

What kind of lives are we building? In our marriage, in our family, in our business, in our churches, in our country? If we work in concert with one another but leave God out, there will never be peace. That may sound hopeless, but let's examine how we can be different.

God's People Embrace the Alternative

In the midst of this indictment of Babylon, God has a message for His people:

"I heard another voice from heaven, saying, 'Come out of her, my people, so that you will not participate in her sins and receive of her plagues...'" Revelation 18:4 (NASB)

We may have to live in Babylon, but Babylon doesn't have to live in us. We are to live the alternative. We are to speak the truth in love. We are to be salt and light.

God gives us hope as we read about the story of Babel retold in the book of Acts.

"The counterpart of the story of the Tower of Babel is the event of Pentecost which is recounted in the New Testament. Here the common language is suddenly present again, and the Parthians, the Medes, and the Elamites understand one another. Here the spell is broken and all the confusion banished." Helmut Thielicke, German Theologian (63)

Babel took place in Babylon—the Anti-God city.	Pentecost took place in Jerusalem—the city of God.
In Babel, the nations gathered together to gain power over God.	In Jerusalem, there were God-fearing people gathered from all the nations in one place to receive God's power.
In Babel, they went from understanding to confusion.	At Pentecost, they went from confusion to understanding.
In Babel, they were building their own empire.	At Pentecost, they were going to build God's Kingdom.
In Babel, they tried to build a gateway to heaven.	At Pentecost, God Himself is the gateway to heaven.
In Babel, one language turned into many so that people can't understand one	At Pentecost, each person heard the message in his or her own native tongue.

another.	
In Babel, they came together and then were scattered.	At Pentecost, they gathered together so they could then be scattered to share the Gospel.

What God did to thwart the plans of the wicked was to break up their ability to understand each other and organize together. But in His Church, God says, "Your diversity is your bond!" God reverses Babel for His people. We have this tremendous unity to work together as God's Church so that we can reach all kinds of people.

At the very end of Genesis 11, God chooses a family through which that "promised seed" of the woman would rise (Genesis 3:15) so that the seed would rise up and crush the serpent's head. And He would deal the fatal blow to the Enemy.

"Now these are the records of the descendants of Terah. Terah was the father of Abram (Abraham), Nahor, and Haran; and Haran was the father of Lot. Haran died before his father Terah in the land of his birth, in [d]Ur of the Chaldeans. Abram and Nahor took wives for themselves. The name of Abram's wife was Sarai (later called Sarah) ...and they went out together to go from Ur of the Chaldeans into the land of Canaan..." Genesis 11: 27-31

"While we were still helpless [powerless to provide for our salvation], at the right time Christ died [as a substitute] for the ungodly." Romans 5:6 (AMP)

The story ends with hope. It's our message. It's Jesus Christ! My King is on the throne. And we believe in a future that is secure.

I pray you will know Jesus Christ, the remarkable wonder of His Person, experience the power of His resurrection, and have fellowship with him.

"And this, so that I may know Him [experientially, becoming more thoroughly acquainted with Him, understanding the remarkable wonders of His Person more completely] and [in that same way experience] the power of His resurrection [which overflows and is active in believers], and [that I may share] the fellowship of His sufferings, by being continually conformed [inwardly into His likeness even] to His death [dying as He did];" Philippians 3:10 (AMP)

Know that God has a plan for you—not to harm you—but a plan to give you a future and a hope.

"'For I know the plans I have for you' declares the Lord, 'plans to prosper you and not to harm you, plans to give you hope and a future.'" Jeremiah 29:11 (NIV)

Growing Roots Deeper
Chapter 11 Questions for Bible Study

1. In the final chapter of this study of Genesis, we learn "... the whole world had one _____ and a common _____." Genesis 11:1 (NIV) Page 141

2. Noah's sons and their offspring scattered and between the Tigris and Euphrates, built a _____ with bricks. Page 141

3. The tower (Ziggurats) was supposed to represent a mountain where the _____ were thought to gather. Page 142

4. In building this tower, these off-springs of Noah were redefining _____. Page 142

5. What is the spirit of Babel? Page 142

6. What four root sins are shown in the building of the Tower of Babel? Page 143

7. The most important part of Genesis 11:1-9 is ___ _____ _____ _____ Page 144

8. Why did He limit progress? Page 144-145

9. In order to limit the _____, God had to break up the _____ and the _____.
Page 145

10. Babylon or Babel is second in importance only to Jerusalem. How are they contrasted on Page 145?

11. How does understanding the spirit of Babel or Babylon help us understand the world today? Page 146

12. Babylon is about _____. It's about uniting a culture against God's values. Page 146

13. _____ God's values. _____ God's values. Page 146

14. Revelation 17-18 deals with the ultimate _____ of Babylon. Page 146

15. In the 404 verses in the book of Revelation and 500 references to the Old Testament, how does the Old Testament help us to understand where the Mark of the Beast will be? Page 147

16. Page 147 states, "To be marked on your forehead is about your _____ and your attitude. If you

are marked on your hand, it's about _____ ___ __.

17. This sign says that my thinking and my behavior match up with the faithfulness of God." Therefore, the Mark of the Beast is about what? Page 147

18. We may have to live in _____, but _____ doesn't have to live in us. We are to live the alternative. We are to speak the _____ in _____. We are to be _____ and _____. Page 148

19. List some contrasts between Babel in Babylon and Pentecost in Jerusalem: Pages 148-149

20. At the very end of Genesis 11, God chooses a family through which that "promised seed" of the woman would rise. Page 149-150 tell us the story ends with hope. Who is that Hope?

21. Know that God has a plan for ___—not to harm ___ —but a plan to give ____ a future and a hope. Page 150

22. Was there a time when you knew God had planned your life? Did it give you hope? When? How?

Footnotes for Chapter 11

60. http://www.beliefnet.com/quotes/inspiration/a/anne-lamott/you-can-safely-assume-youve-created-god-in-your-o.aspxJohn Walton, Genesis: The NIV Application Commentary. (Grand Rapids, MI: Zondervan, 2001) 466.
61. John Walton, Genesis: The NIV Application Commentary. (Grand Rapids, MI: Zondervan, 2001) 466
62. Gordon J. Wenham, "Genesis 1-15" Word Biblical Commentary (Waco, TX: Word, 1987), 235.
63. Helmut Thielicke, How the World Began: Man in the First Chapters of the Bible (Philadelphia, PA, Muhlenberg Press, 1961), 276.

ABOUT THE AUTHOR

Born in New Orleans, Louisiana, Dr. Mark Forrest grew up as the oldest child in an unchurched family. Soon after his parents divorced, his mom moved the family to Shreveport, Louisiana, where the students at Haughton High School shared the Gospel with Mark. He embraced the love of Christ, believed and was baptized on November 8, 1980.

As an active member of the Baptist Student Union in Louisiana State University-Shreveport, he discovered a love for teaching and preaching. During his senior year, he sensed a calling to serve in full-time ministry. He met Gina DiMaria at the Baptist Student Union and they were married in 1989. Gina grew up being involved in her parents' ministry including a church camp and a television ministry.

After college, Mark and Gina moved to Fort Worth, Texas, where he pursued a Master of Divinity degree. Upon the completion of that degree, they moved to Malawi, Africa with their 6-month-old daughter to work with churches. In Malawi, Mark served as an administrator of a medical clinic. After their two-year commitment, they moved back to Texas, and with help from his wife and their six children, Mark began a pastor's journey. During this time Mark earned a Doctor of Ministry degree at Southwestern Seminary. With twenty-three years as a pastoral family, they currently serve at Lakeside Baptist Church in Granbury, Texas.

Pre-order Mark's next book, *Revelations – a Love Story*.

Visit Pastor Mark's Amazon author page and leave him a comment. He loves to hear from friends, old and new.

Notes

Notes

Made in the USA
Lexington, KY
09 December 2018